# Personal Expressions

## Writing Your Way into English

# Personal Expressions

## Writing Your Way into English

**Susan J. Dicker**

**Hostos Community College
City University of New York**

Heinle & Heinle Publishers
A Division of Wadsworth, Inc.
Boston, Massachusetts 02116 U.S.A.

## ACKNOWLEDGMENTS

This textbook would never have seen the light of day without the inspiration of my friend and colleague David Blot. Together with another colleague, Socorro de Jesus, we came up with the idea for this book during the summer discussions in which we searched for ways to better serve our students at Hostos Community College, CUNY. I owe a huge debt to the students at Hostos, whose passionate voices I sought to re-create in the stories told here. I also thank all those colleagues who read early versions of the text and tested them at their colleges, especially Mel Baron of Kingsborough Community College, CUNY, whose encouragement and friendship will be remembered always.

*Personal Expressions*

Copyright © 1992 by Heinle & Heinle Publishers

All rights reserved. No part of this publication may be reproduced or transmitted in any form or by any means, electronic, or mechanical, including photocopy, recording, or any information storage and retrieval system, without permission in writing from the publisher.

Heinle & Heinle Publishers is a division of Wadsworth, Inc.

Manufactured in the United States of America

Publisher: Stanley J. Galek

Editor: Erik Gundersen

Associate Editor: Lynne Telson Barsky

Editorial Production Manager: Elizabeth Holthaus

Production Editor: Kristin M. Thalheimer

Manufacturing Coordinator: Jerry Christopher

Interior and Cover Design and Composition: Greta D. Sibley

Cover Background Art: Diane E. Daniel

Library of Congress Cataloging-in-Publication Data

Dicker, Susan J.
    Personal expressions • writing your way into English / Susan J. Dicker
      p. cm.
    ISBN 0-8384-3014-7 :
    1. English language — Rhetoric. 2. English language — Textbooks for foreign speakers. I. Title.
PE1408.D49 1992
808'.042—dc20

91-43001
CIP

ISBN 0-8384-3014-7

10 9 8 7 6 5 4 3 2 1

*Dedicated to the memory of my parents,
Leo and Melinda Dicker,
who were the first and most important ESL learners
in my life.*

# Preface

### RATIONALE

The purpose of PERSONAL EXPRESSIONS is to introduce high-beginning college and adult ESL students to the art of writing. Students who are able to give information about themselves and express opinions in simple oral and written statements should be ready to tackle this text.

The focus of the writing activities is on personal experience, a natural starting point for writing as well as for language learning in general. I believe that this goal serves adults learning in both college and adult education settings. Those learners who are not pursuing a college degree acquire the skills and satisfaction of expressing themselves well to others. For those who are in college, the basics of writing learned here will serve them well when they reach higher-level ESL and English composition courses.

The sequence of themes in PERSONAL EXPRESSIONS proceeds from writing about what is closest to the students' lives to writing about the world around them and how that world affects them. This sequence will prepare students to write about more abstract concepts in the future.

Most college students are also required to take a minimum-competency writing test. Often, this test asks students to support a point of view on a particular topic with examples from their own lives. This book helps prepare students for the challenges of effectively taking such a test.

## ORGANIZATION OF THE TEXT

The chapters and lessons in PERSONAL EXPRESSIONS are arranged thematically. At the core of each lesson are two sample student compositions which present both good models of writing and timely issues for discussion. The exercises after each composition ask students to note new vocabulary words, react to and analyze what they have read, and, finally, to relate these powerful stories to their own lives. Students are encouraged to share their written responses with each other.

The two compositions in each lesson are followed by a *Focus* section. Here, a language structure or function which arises naturally in the readings is explained, followed by exercises for practice. It is important to note the role that grammar and structure play in this text. Many textbooks are organized around a carefully ordered grammatical syllabus; readings or sample compositions are used to initiate explanations and exercises on the grammatical points in the syllabus. Unlike these texts, PERSONAL EXPRESSIONS is arranged thematically; its goal is to get students to write thoughtful compositions about their lives. A necessary step in reaching this goal is paying attention to grammatical and structural accuracy. To this end, the *Focus* sections concentrate on some of the discrete points of language which are often problematic at this level.

The final section of each lesson, *Pulling It Together,* emphasizes small group work. Students read the compositions to each other to practice pronunciation and to make links between oral and written English. A series of exercises leads students to choose a theme to write on, and then to generate details about that theme. Next, students work on their own to write their compositions. Finally, drafts of student writing are read in groups for peer feedback before they are handed in to the teacher.

## PROCESS WRITING

Following the composing-process theory of teaching writing, PERSONAL EXPRESSIONS encourages students to write multiple drafts and to concentrate on different aspects of language with each revision. It is important to note, however, that I have refrained from imposing a rigid set of rules for students to follow. I believe that the writing process should be fluid, flexible, and adaptable to different students at different stages of language development. Instead of teaching one preferred way to edit and revise one's writing, I offer several different ways in Appendix I entitled *Revising Guidelines*.

Each section of Appendix I discusses an important aspect of writing appropriate for high-beginning students, ranging from the larger concerns of theme and organization to more specific structural and grammatical matters. A technique for analyzing each aspect of writing in one's own composition is offered along with a practice exercise. If the teacher requires additional exercises, he or she may ask the class to apply the revising technique to copies of student writing or to sample compositions. When most of the students appear comfortable with the technique, they can then begin to apply it to their own writing.

PERSONAL EXPRESSIONS provides teachers with a great deal of flexibility in teaching the writing process. Teachers using the book are free to decide when and how to introduce each technique for revising. Knowledge of his or her students should also allow each teacher to decide whether revising should be done individually, in pairs, or in groups.

Appendix 2 is entitled *Supplementary Material.* Since many high-beginning ESL students may be unfamiliar with grammatical terminology, Appendix 2 is devoted largely to explaining the terms used in the body of the text. This appendix also includes exercises designed to diagnose students' understanding of the terms. A section on irregular verbs in the simple past and in the participle form and a section on spelling rules for adding *-s, -ed,* and *-ing* are also included, along with the diagnostic exercises. Teachers should refer students to this appendix at any appropriate time while using the text.

# Contents

**Preface** .................................................................... vi

**Chapter One: Describing Feelings** ............................................. 1

   **Lesson 1: The First Day of Class** .......................................... 2
      *First-Day Jitters*
      *A Confident Student*
   Focus: Expressing the Present and the Future ........................... 7
   Pulling It Together ..................................................... 10

   **Lesson 2: Feelings about People** ......................................... 12
      *A Wonderful Boy*
      *My Best Friend*
   Focus: Gerunds and Infinitives as Secondary Verbs ...................... 17
   Pulling It Together ..................................................... 20

**Chapter Two: Recalling Past Experiences** .................................... 21

   **Lesson 1: An Important Day** .............................................. 22
      *A Beautiful Wedding*
      *When My Grandmother Died*
   Focus: The Simple Past Tense; The Uses of *And* ........................ 26
   Pulling It Together ..................................................... 30

**Lesson 2: Learning How** ...................................................32
    *Swimming Lessons*
    *Teaching Myself to Cook*
  Focus: Direct and Reported Speech............................................36
  Pulling It Together .......................................................................40

**Chapter Three: Midsemester Progress Report** .....................43
  What Am I Doing Right? What Am I Doing Wrong? ............44
  Getting Better Every Day ..........................................................46
  Pulling It Together .......................................................................48

**Chapter Four: Influences on My Life** ....................................49

**Lesson 1: A Person Who Has Influenced Me** ...................50
    *A Model Woman*
    *A Different Kind of Father*
  Focus: *It + Be + Adjective* ........................................................54
  Pulling It Together .......................................................................56

**Lesson 2: An Event That Has Influenced Me** ...................59
    *Losing a Friend to Drugs*
    *A Story of Prejudice*
  Focus: The Present Perfect and Past Perfect Tenses ............65
  Pulling It Together .......................................................................69

**Chapter Five: Imagining** ............................................................71

**Lesson 1: In My Favorite Place** ............................................72
    *Central Park*
    *In My Backyard*
  Focus: *There + Be + Noun* .......................................................78
  Pulling It Together .......................................................................81

**Lesson 2: Change of Identity** ...............................................83
    *Rock Star*
    *Mayor*
  Focus: Gerund and Infinitive Phrases .......................................89
  Pulling It Together .......................................................................91

**Chapter Six: Last Words** ..........................................................94

**Appendix 1: Revising Guidelines ..................................................96**

    1. Selecting a Title ..................................................................96
    2. Thematic Consistency ........................................................97
    3. Paragraphing.....................................................................100
    4. Punctuation ......................................................................105
    5. Subject-Verb Agreement..................................................109
    6. Verb Tense Consistency ...................................................110

**Appendix 2: Supplementary Material ..................................115**

    1. Parts of Speech: Nouns, Adjectives, Verbs, Adverbs .....115
    2. Noun and Adjective Clauses............................................117
    3. The Parts of a Sentence ..................................................118
    4. Pronouns..........................................................................120
    5. Auxiliaries ........................................................................122
    6. Irregular Verbs .................................................................124
    7. Spelling Rules for Adding *-s, -ed* and *-ing*................................126

# CHAPTER ONE

# Describing Feelings

**Lesson 1:** The First Day of Class

*First-Day Jitters*

*A Confident Student*

Focus: Expressing the Present and the Future

**Lesson 2:** Feelings about People

*A Wonderful Boy*

*My Best Friend*

Focus: Gerunds and Infinitives as Secondary Verbs

# LESSON ONE The First Day of Class

### First-Day Jitters

It's Monday morning. It's the first day of the new semester. This is a very special day for me.

This is my second semester of college. I'm starting a new ESL class. I am excited because I'm going to meet my new teacher. I hope that I will like the teacher. I'm also going to meet my new classmates. I hope that some of them will become my friends.

I am also a little nervous today. I hope this class will not be too difficult. I hope I will have time to do all of my homework because I work every afternoon after school. I want to be a good student and I want to get a good grade.

*(This story was written by Mohammed.)*

**THINKING ABOUT THE STORY**

1. Write three sentences from the story. Choose sentences that you like for some reason.

    a. _____

    b. _____

    c. _____

2. Which of these three sentences do you like the best: (a), (b), or (c)? Write it again here.

3. Why do you like that sentence? Choose one of the following reasons and write it on the lines below.

    a. It contains interesting information.

    b. It has new vocabulary that I want to learn.

    c. It contains information that reminds me of my own life.

    d. It has some words that I want to learn how to spell.

    e. I want to learn how to express myself the same way.

3

4. Write two more sentences from the story. Choose sentences that do not remind you of your own life.

   a. _____
   _____
   _____

   b. _____
   _____
   _____

5. Now change those two sentences so that they give information about your own life.

   a. _____
   _____
   _____

   b. _____
   _____
   _____

6. Finish these sentences so that they express the way you feel today.

   a. Today I feel _____ because
   _____
   _____

   b. I hope that _____
   _____
   _____

   c. I want to _____
   _____
   _____

## A Confident Student

It's Thursday morning. It's the first day of the new semester. This is a very special day for me.

This is my fourth semester of college. I'm starting a new ESL class. I'm excited because I'm going to meet my new teacher, and I hope I will like him or her. I know some of the students who are in my class. They are already my friends. I am excited about seeing them again after the summer vacation.

Last year I was nervous on the first day of class, but now I feel more confident. I know that every year my English improves a little more. Now I also know how to organize my time so that I can study. Every afternoon, I spend two hours studying and doing my homework before I get ready to go to work. That way, I am always prepared for class the next day. I know I will get a good grade this semester.

*(This composition was written by Manuel.)*

**THINKING ABOUT THE STORY**

1. Write one sentence from the story. Choose the sentence that you like the best.

   _____
   _____

2. Why do you like that sentence? Choose one of the following reasons and write it on the lines below.

   a. It expresses the way I feel.
   b. It expresses the way that I want to feel.
   c. It contains interesting information.
   d. It has vocabulary that I want to learn.
   e. It has some words that I want to learn how to spell.

   _____
   _____

3. Write two more sentences from the story. Choose sentences that do not remind you of your own life.

   a. _____
   _____

   b. _____
   _____

4. Now change those two sentences so that they give information about your own life.

   a. _____
   _____

   b. _____
   _____

5. Write three things you will do this semester so that you will have time to study.

   This semester I will _____

   _____. I will _____

   _____. In addition, I will _____ .

6. What are some of things you can do to practice your English in general? How can you study what you learn in class? Finish these paragraphs.

To practice English, I can listen to English songs. I can _____ _____. I can _____ _____. I can also _____ _____.

To study what I learn in class, I can practice reading the stories in the book at home. I can _____. I can _____ _____. I can also _____ _____.

As the semester progresses, find other ways to study and practice English. Talk to other students to find out what they do.

## FOCUS: EXPRESSING THE PRESENT AND THE FUTURE

**Expressing the Present**

**Simple Present Tense.** The simple present tense is used in Lesson 1 to describe a mental or emotional state.

   I *hope* that I will like the teacher.
   I *want* to be a good student.

Another way to express a mental or emotional state is to use the verb *be* and an adjective.

   I*'m* excited, because I'm going to meet my new teacher.
   I *am* also a little nervous.
   I *am* always prepared for class the next day.

We also use the simple present tense to describe an activity that is habitual, that takes place repeatedly in the present.

   Every afternoon, I *spend* two hours studying and doing my homework before I *get* ready to go to work.

**Present Continuous.** The present continuous is used to describe something that is happening at this moment.

Right now, *I'm reading* about verb tenses.

It can also be used to describe something that is happening in someone's life over a general period of time in the present.

*I'm starting* a new ESL class.
This semester, *I'm working* at a drugstore.

**Exercise 1.** With each verb below, write a sentence about yourself in the simple present. Then write a sentence in the present continuous with the verb.

> **Example:**
> make  *I make breakfast every morning.*
>             *I'm making a lot of friends at college.*

1. study _____

2. talk _____

3. listen _____

4. write _____

5. read _____

**Exercise 2.** Choose five of the following adjectives and write a sentence for each, expressing how you feel. Use *I am* or *I'm* in your sentences.

| | | | | |
|---|---|---|---|---|
| excited | unhappy | nervous | prepared | happy |
| comfortable | confused | worried | | |

8

> **Example:**
> *I'm comfortable in this class because some of my friends are here.*

1. _____

2. _____

3. _____

4. _____

5. _____

## Expressing the Future

***Will* + Infinitive.*** In the stories in Lesson 1, the future is often expressed by using *will* and an infinitive verb.

I hope *I will like* the teacher.

I hope this class *will not be* too difficult.

***Be* + *Going to* + Infinitive.*** Another way to express the future is to use *be* + *going to* and an infinitive verb. Here is an example from Manuel's story.

I am excited because *I'm going to meet* my new teacher.

**Exercise.** Complete the two paragraphs below. In the first, write about your plans for next week. In the second, write about your plans for the future. For practice, use *be + going to + infinitive* in the first paragraph and *will + infinitive* in the second paragraph. Write five sentences for each paragraph. Here are some ideas.

| | | |
|---|---|---|
| go to a party | have a good time | get married |
| go out to dinner | visit a relative | cook dinner |
| return to my country | buy a house | get a good job |

Next week I'm going to _____

_____

_____

_____

_____

_____

_____

In the future, I will _____

_____

_____

_____

_____

_____

_____

## PULLING IT TOGETHER

1. Do the following exercises in a group of three or four students.

   a. Read "First-Day Jitters" and "A Confident Student" in your group. One student will read the first story aloud and another student will read the second story. As you listen to your classmates read, write down any words that you think are mispronounced. Discuss these words after each classmate has finished reading.

   b. Discuss with your classmates how Mohammed and Manuel are similar and how they are different. Then complete these paragraphs.

Mohammed and Manuel are similar in some ways. They are both college students. _____
_____
_____
_____
_____

Mohammed and Manuel are different in some ways. Mohammed is in his second semester of college and Manuel is in his fourth semester. _____
_____
_____
_____
_____

c. As a student who is starting a new ESL class, who do you identify with more, Mohammed or Manuel? Explain your answer to the students in your group. Then write a short explanation in the space below.

   I identify with _____ because _____
   _____
   _____
   _____ .

2. You will now write your own story. Because it may not be the first day of class anymore, you can (a) pretend it's the first day of class now, or (b) describe how you feel about your class now.

3. Write as many drafts of your composition as necessary. With your teacher, decide which areas in the Appendix 1, *Revising Guidelines,* you should concentrate on at each step in writing your story. You may revise your paper alone or with the help of one or two classmates, according to your teacher's instructions.

4. When you have written your final draft, get together with your group and read your story aloud. Listen to questions or suggestions from your classmates. Make any final changes that you think are necessary.

# LESSON TWO Feelings about People

### A Wonderful Boy

My son is the most important person in my life. He is a wonderful boy.

My son's name is Paolo. He is four years old. He is small for his age. He has big brown eyes and straight black hair. He is a very playful child. He likes to run and jump and play games with other children. He enjoys going to the park and to the movies. Most of the time he obeys me, but sometimes he does things that I don't like. Sometimes he walks into the street alone or gets into fights with other children, and I have to punish him. However, he is usually a good and affectionate boy. He often stops playing to get a hug or a kiss from me.

Paolo goes to a day-care center. He is learning to read and write. He is very intelligent and I am proud of him. He is growing up very quickly, but he still depends on me for everything in his life. I am going to college so that I can get a job and give Paolo the things he needs.

I love Paolo very much. I am taking very good care of him because I want him to grow up to be a happy and successful person.

## THINKING ABOUT THE STORY

1. Write three sentences from the story that you like.

    a. _____

    b. _____

    c. _____

2. Write three sentences from the story that have words or expressions that are new to you. Circle those words or expressions.

    a. _____

    b. _____

    c. _____

3. Write the new words on the lines below. Find out what they mean from the teacher, another student, or the dictionary. Write the meanings in English or in your native language. Also write the part of speech; for example, noun, adjective (adj.), verb, adverb (adv.).

| Word or Expression | Meaning | Part of Speech |
| --- | --- | --- |
|  |  |  |
|  |  |  |
|  |  |  |
|  |  |  |
|  |  |  |
|  |  |  |
|  |  |  |

4. Finish these sentences to describe a male child that you know (for example, son, nephew, brother, grandson, friend's son).

My _____ is _____ years old.
    (son, nephew, etc.)   (number)

He is _____ and _____ .
     (adjective)        (adjective)

He has _____ hair. He likes to _____ .
     (adjective)             (verb)

5. Finish the sentence below, referring to a child that you know. Write two or three sentences.

I love my _____ because _____

_____

_____

_____

_____

_____

_____

_____

_____ .

## My Best Friend

My mother is a very important person in my life. She is my best friend. I depend on her love and support.

My mother is fifty-two years old. She is short and chubby and she has curly blond hair. She is a very lively person. She likes to go out to eat, to the movies, and dancing. Everyone enjoys being with her because she likes to have a good time. She is a good friend to many people. When her neighbors are sick, she is always the first one to visit them, bringing some good food that she made. People always come to her with their problems, and she is always ready to help them.

My mother lives in Israel. Even though I live far away from her, I feel very close to her. I call her on the phone whenever I have a problem or I feel sad. She listens to me and talks to me, and then I feel better. Every year my children and I go to visit her. I help her with her housework because I think she works too hard. We play together with the children. She is a very loving grandmother.

My mother is a wonderful person. I always try to be just like her.

**THINKING ABOUT THE STORY**

1. Write three sentences from the story that you like.

    a. _____

    _____

    b. _____

    _____

    c. _____

    _____

2. Write three sentences from the story that have words or expressions that are new to you. Circle those words or expressions.

    a. _____

    _____

    b. _____

    _____

    c. _____

    _____

3. Write the new words on the lines below. Find out what they mean from the teacher, another student, or the dictionary. Write the meanings in English or in your native language. Also write the part of speech.

| Word or Expression | Meaning | Part of Speech |
| --- | --- | --- |
| _____ | _____ | _____ |
| _____ | _____ | _____ |
| _____ | _____ | _____ |
| _____ | _____ | _____ |
| _____ | _____ | _____ |
| _____ | _____ | _____ |
| _____ | _____ | _____ |

4. Finish these sentences, describing your own mother or a female friend or relative.

   My _____ is _____ years old.
      (mother, sister, etc.)   (number)

   She is _____ and _____ .
       (adjective)     (adjective)

   She likes to _____ . When I am with her, I feel _____ .
        (verb)                               (adjective)

5. Finish the sentence below, referring to someone you admire and want to be like. Choose a relative, like your mother or father, or a friend.

   I want to be like _____ because _____
   _____
   _____
   _____ .

## FOCUS: GERUNDS AND INFINITIVES AS SECONDARY VERBS

Sentences often have more than one verb. The first verb is the main verb, and it is conjugated in the past, present, or future tense. The secondary verb is in the form of a gerund or infinitive. Sentences like these are in Lesson 2.

He enjoys *going* to the park and to the movies. (gerund)

He often stops *playing* to get a hug or a kiss from me. (gerund)

He likes *to run and jump and play* games with other children. (infinitive)

I always try *to be* just like her. (infinitive)

There is no rule that explains why some secondary verbs have to be gerunds and some have to be infinitives. The decision to use a gerund or an infinitive depends on the main verb in the sentence. Here are three lists of commonly used verbs which are followed by a gerund, an infinitive, or either one.

1. Main verbs followed by a gerund:

   | enjoy | finish | give up | keep on |
   |-------|--------|---------|---------|
   | miss | practice | stop | |

   **Examples:**
   I enjoy *dancing and listening* to music.
   I finished *cleaning* the house.

2. Main verbs followed by an infinitive:

   | decide | forget | have | hope | learn |
   |--------|--------|------|------|-------|
   | need | plan | want | want (someone) | would like |

   **Examples:**
   I forgot *to bring* my homework today.
   I want my son *to be* a doctor.

3. Main verbs followed by either a gerund or an infinitive:

   | begin | continue | hate | like | love |
   |-------|----------|------|------|------|
   | prefer | start | try | | |

   **Examples:**
   I began *studying* English three years ago.
   I began *to study* English three years ago.
   I like *watching* horror movies.
   I like *to watch* horror movies.

**Exercise:** Complete the sentences below, using an expression that begins with a secondary verb.

> **Example:** My sister plans *to get a job after college.*

1. Last year I started _____

2. My father enjoys _____

3. I want my family _____

4. Last week I forgot _____

5. I will never stop _____

6. My friend decided _____

7. I always try _____

8. I want my children _____

9. Every night I go to sleep after I finish _____

10. I want to continue _____

**PULLING IT TOGETHER** ..................................................................................

1. Do the following exercises in a group of three or four students.

   a. Read "A Wonderful Boy" and "My Best Friend" in your group. One student will read the first story aloud and another student will read the second story. As you listen to your classmates read, write down any words that you think are mispronounced. Discuss these words after each classmate has finished reading.

   b. Choose a person who is important to you in your life. Describe that person on the lines below, using the questions as a guide. When everyone in the group is finished, share what you wrote with each other.

   1) What does the person look like?

      _____
      _____
      _____

   2) What type of personality does he or she have? Give examples of the person's behavior which demonstrate his or her personality.

      _____
      _____
      _____

   3) Describe the special relationship that you have with this person. Why is he or she important to you?

      _____
      _____
      _____

2. Now write your story about a person who is important in your life. Use ideas from the stories in this section and from the notes you have written above. Write as many drafts of your composition as necessary. With your teacher, decide which areas in Appendix 1, *Revising Guidelines*, you should concentrate on at each step in writing your story. You may revise your paper alone or with the help of one or two classmates, according to your teacher's instructions.

3. When you have written your final draft, get together with your group and read your story aloud. Listen to questions or suggestions from your classmates. Make any final changes that you think are necessary.

# CHAPTER TWO

# Recalling Past Experiences

**Lesson 1:** An Important Day

   *A Beautiful Wedding*

   *When My Grandmother Died*

   Focus: The Simple Past Tense

           The Uses of *And*

**Lesson 2:** Learning How

   *Swimming Lessons*

   *Teaching Myself to Cook*

   Focus: Direct and Reported Speech

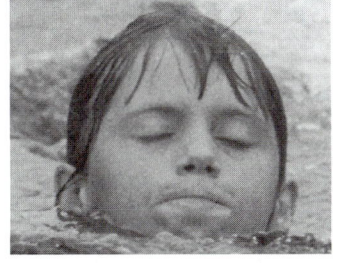

# LESSON ONE  An Important Day

## A Beautiful Wedding

The happiest day of my life was the day I got married. I will never forget that day.

It was a beautiful day in April. I woke up early in the morning. I had my last breakfast with my parents, brothers, and sisters. That made me a little sad. We all got dressed and went to the church. We waited one hour until everyone arrived. Then the wedding ceremony began. It was very beautiful. There were flowers all over the church and someone played music on the church organ. When the priest said that we were married, I started to cry. My husband winked at me and we both laughed.

After the ceremony, we had a reception at my house. All my relatives and friends were there. There was a wonderful orchestra that played our favorite music. Everyone danced a lot. My mother and her friends prepared delicious food, and everyone ate and drank a lot. We all enjoyed it very much.

I was very happy with my husband on that day. Now we have two children and we are still happy. I always remember that special day when we began our wonderful life together.

**THINKING ABOUT THE STORY**

1. Do you like this story? Why or why not? Answer with one or two sentences. Cross out *like* or *don't like* and leave the word or words that express how you feel.

   I like/don't like this story because _____
   _____
   _____
   _____.

2. List any words or expressions from the story that are new to you. Find out what they mean from the teacher, another student, or the dictionary. Then write the meanings in English or in your native language. Also write the part of speech.

   | Word or Expression | Meaning | Part of Speech |
   | --- | --- | --- |
   | _____ | _____ | _____ |
   | _____ | _____ | _____ |
   | _____ | _____ | _____ |

3. Pretend that you are the writer's brother, sister, mother, or father. Describe how you felt on the day of the wedding and recall some of the memories you have of that day.

   I remember the day that my _____ got married. _____
   _____
   _____
   _____
   _____
   _____
   _____
   _____
   _____

4. Share what you wrote with a classmate.

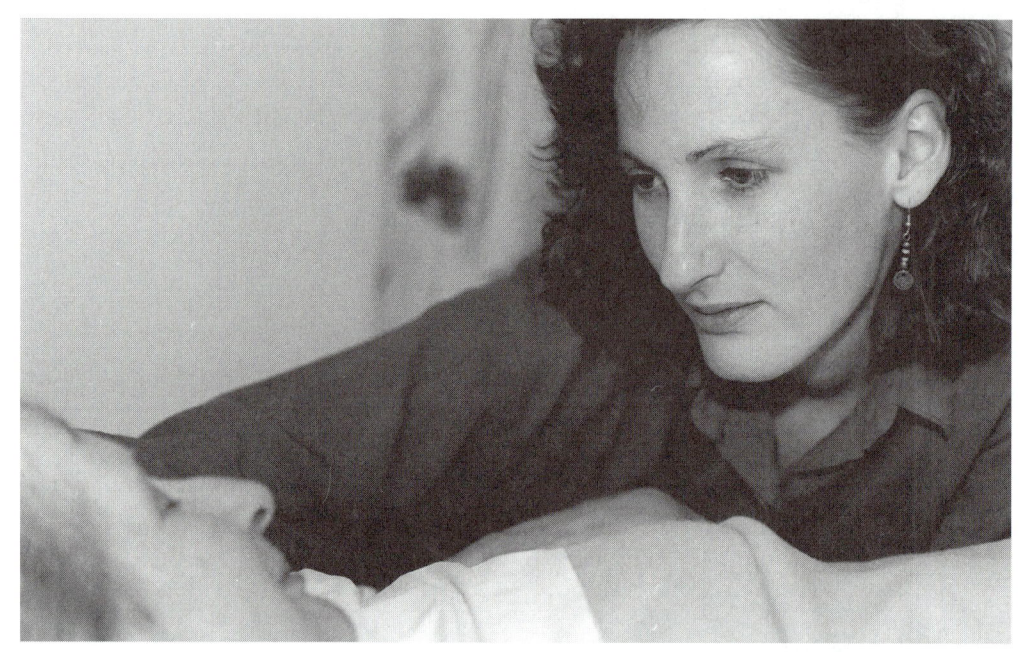

## When My Grandmother Died

The worst day of my life was the day my grandmother died. It was a very sad time for me.

I remember that I was at work that day. I got a phone call from my brother, who told me that my grandmother was very ill. I finished my work and went to the hospital, hoping that she was still alive.

When I got to the hospital, my whole family was in the room with my grandmother. Everyone was crying. I went to my grandmother's bed and I talked to her. I told her that I loved her and that she was a wonderful grandmother. I hoped that she could hear me, but she didn't say anything to me. Two hours later she died.

My father told us that we shouldn't be too sad because my grandmother lived a long and happy life. However, I still feel a little guilty because I never told her how much I loved her when she was still alive.

## THINKING ABOUT THE STORY

1. How does this story make you feel, and why? Answer in one or two sentences.

    This story makes me feel _____ because _____
    _____
    _____.

2. List any words or expressions that are new to you. Find out what they mean and write the meanings in English or in your native language. Also write the part of speech.

| Word or Expression | Meaning | Part of Speech |
|---|---|---|
| _____ | _____ | _____ |
| _____ | _____ | _____ |
| _____ | _____ | _____ |

3. Do you remember a time when you felt guilty about something that you did or didn't do? Explain on the lines below.

    _____
    _____
    _____
    _____
    _____
    _____
    _____
    _____
    _____
    _____
    _____
    _____
    _____

4. Share what you wrote with a classmate.

## FOCUS: THE SIMPLE PAST TENSE; THE USES OF *AND*

### The Simple Past Tense

When you recall a sequence of events that happened in your life, use the simple past tense form of the main verbs. For most verbs, this tense is formed by adding *-ed* or *-d* to the end of the verb. See Spelling Rules, page 126 in Appendix 2, *Supplementary Material,* for more information. Here are examples from the stories of sentences with regular past tense verbs.

We *waited* one hour until everyone *arrived*.
We all *enjoyed* it very much.

You can find a list of irregular past tense verbs on page 124 in Appendix 2, *Supplementary Material.* Here are examples from the stories of sentences with irregular past tense verbs.

I *woke up* early in the morning.
After the ceremony, we *had* a reception at my house.
I *got* a phone call from my brother.

In order to form a negative past tense verb, use the word *didn't* and the infinitive form of the verb. This is true for all verbs. Here is an example.

I hoped that she could hear me, but she *didn't say* anything to me.

**Exercise.** The verbs in the following paragraph are in the future tense. First, read the paragraph and underline all the future tense main verbs. Then, rewrite the paragraph in the past tense. The first sentence is done for you.

Next Saturday, I *will visit* my Uncle Dimitris. I will arrive at his apartment at 12:30 P.M. We will sit in the kitchen and have a cup of coffee. Then, we will take a walk in the park. We will watch the children playing baseball. After that, we will go to a nice restaurant for lunch. I will try to pay for the lunch, but Uncle Dimitris will not want me to. He will ask the waiter for the check and he will pay for our lunch. Then, we will look at the newspaper and decide on a movie. After the movie, we will not go directly home. I will walk with Uncle Dimitris to his friend Joe's house. Dimitris and Joe will begin a game of cards. I will go home.

Last Saturday, I visited my Uncle Dimitris.

## The Uses of *and*

The word *and* is used to add two or more words or phrases of any grammatical category: nouns and noun phrases; adjectives and adjective phrases; verbs; and whole sentences. Here are examples from the stories:

I had my last breakfast with *my parents, brothers,* AND *sisters.*
*(noun phrase) (noun) (noun)*

I *finished* my work AND *went* to the hospital.
*(verb) (verb)*

My grandmother lived a *long* AND *happy* life.
*(adj.) (adj.)*

*My husband winked at me* AND *we both laughed.*
*(sentence) (sentence)*

In the above examples, notice that verbs linked with *and* have the same form (*finished* and *went*, *winked* and *laughed*). Here are other examples:

We enjoy *fishing* and *hiking*.

He will *finish* the dishes and then *go* to bed.

It is incorrect to add two words or phrases that are not of the same grammatical category. For example, this sentence is incorrect.

   She is *pretty* and    *long hair.*
      (adj.)     (noun phrase)

The sentence is correct like this.

   She  *is*  pretty and  *has*  long hair.
      (verb)       (verb)

When you add only two words or two short phrases together, you do not use a comma before *and*.

   *She is strong and intelligent.*

If you are adding two long phrases or sentences, you may use a comma before *and* or you may leave the comma out. Look at these sentences.

   I have red hair, and my brother has blond hair.
                  *or*
   I have red hair and my brother has blond hair.

When adding three or more words or phrases together with *and,* you must use a comma between every pair of words or phrases except the last two, which are joined by *and*. (A comma before *and* is preferred, but it is optional.) Look at the use of commas in these series of words.

   eggs, cheese, butter, milk and coffee
              *or*
   eggs, cheese, butter, milk, and coffee

> **Exercise 1.** Combine each set of sentences into one sentence, using *and*.
>
> > **Example:** My sister is smart. My sister is funny. My sister is pretty.
> >
> > *My sister is smart, funny, and pretty.*

1. He had two notebooks in his briefcase. He had four textbooks in his briefcase. He had a dictionary in his briefcase.

   _____
   _____

2. We had a picnic lunch.  We swam in the ocean.  We tried to get a suntan.

3. Julia bought a new dress for herself.  Julia bought a shirt for her son.

4. I want my son to be a doctor.  I want my daughter to be a lawyer.

5. George is studying to be a computer programmer.  His wife wants to teach kindergarten.

**Exercise 2.** Using the sentences from Exercise 1 as models, write five sentences about your own life.  Use *and* to connect two or more words or phrases.

> **Example (from number 1):** I have three textbooks, one notebook, and five pencils in my book bag.

1. 
2. 
3. 
4. 
5.

## PULLING IT TOGETHER

1. Do the following exercises in a group of three or four students.

   a. Read "A Beautiful Wedding" and "When My Grandmother Died" in your group. One student will read the first story and another student will read the second story. As you listen to your classmates read, write down any words that you think are mispronounced. Discuss these words after each classmate has finished reading.

   b. Look at the two lists below. One is a list of events that you may have experienced in the past. The other is a list of feelings. Choose one event that you have experienced. Which feeling or feelings do you associate with this event? (If you want to, add events and feelings to the lists.) After choosing one event, complete the sentences below. Share what you wrote with your group.

   | Events | Feelings |
   | --- | --- |
   | the day I got married | excited |
   | the day I graduated from high school | nervous |
   | the day I left my country | wonderful |
   | the day my spouse and I decided to get married | afraid |
   | the day I arrived in the United States | worried |
   | the day a relative or friend died | angry |
   | the day my child was born | guilty |
   | my first day of school | confident |
   | the day my divorce became final | confused |
   | | proud |

   The day I _____,

   I felt _____ because _____
   _____.

   I also felt _____

   because _____.

c. Try to remember that day as clearly as you can. Close your eyes and think of all the details about that day. What was the weather like? What were you wearing? What were other people wearing? What were other people saying about the event? If it was a celebration, what did you do? Did you go somewhere special? Did you eat or drink something special? On the lines below, write down some quick notes on as many details as you can remember.

_____
_____
_____
_____
_____
_____
_____
_____
_____
_____
_____
_____
_____

d. Share what you have written with the other members of your group. Try to get ideas for different types of details from other students in your group.

2. Now write your story. Include as many details about that day as you can remember. Write as many drafts as necessary. With your teacher, decide which areas in Appendix 1, *Revising Guidelines,* you should concentrate on at each step in writing your story. You may revise your paper alone or with the help of one or two other classmates, according to your teacher's instructions.

3. When you have written your final draft, get together with your group and read your story aloud. Listen to questions or suggestions from your classmates. Make any final changes you think are necessary.

# LESSON TWO

# Learning How

### Swimming Lessons

When I was a little boy, I was afraid of the water. When my family went to the beach, I was the only one who wouldn't go into the ocean. I was a little embarrassed about this because all my brothers, sisters, and friends could swim.

One summer, when I was eight, my uncle came to visit us. We went to the beach one Saturday, and he was surprised to learn that I couldn't swim yet. He asked me, "Why are you afraid of the water?" I didn't really have an answer. He said, "I'll teach you how to swim." I told him that I didn't want to do it in front of all the people at the beach.

So, every morning he took me to the swimming pool at the house of one of his friends. I started by going into the shallow part of the pool. My uncle taught me how to float. I practiced moving my arms and legs while he held me with his hands. When I became more confident, we went into the deeper end of the pool. After about a month I knew how to swim.

Then one day we were all at the beach. I surprised everyone by going into the water. The water felt cool and refreshing because it was a hot day. I started to swim and everyone applauded. I wasn't afraid of the ocean anymore. I always remember my uncle because he taught me a wonderful thing: how to swim.

**THINKING ABOUT THE STORY**

1. Do you like this story? Why or why not? Answer in two or three sentences. Cross out *like* or *don't like* and leave the word or words that express how you feel.

   I like/don't like this story because _____
   _____
   _____
   _____.

2. List any words or expressions from the story that are new to you. Find out what they mean and write the meanings in English or in your native language. Also write the part of speech.

   | Word or Expression | Meaning | Part of Speech |
   | --- | --- | --- |
   | _____ | _____ | _____ |
   | _____ | _____ | _____ |
   | _____ | _____ | _____ |
   | _____ | _____ | _____ |

3. Did anyone in your life ever teach you how to do something special? Did you ever teach someone else how to do something special? How did it make you feel? Finish the sentences below so that they are true for you.

   a. My _____ taught me how to _____
   _____.

   I felt very _____.

   b. My _____ taught me how to _____
   _____.

   I felt very _____.

   c. I taught my _____ how to _____
   _____.

   This made me feel _____.

33

### Teaching Myself to Cook

When I was a little girl growing up in Italy, my mother did all the cooking. I got married when I was seventeen. My husband expected me to make all the meals, but I didn't know how.

The first night that I had to cook for my husband, I decided to make a fish soup called *suppa di frutti di mare* in Italian. This is a very complicated dish that my mother used to make very often. However, I couldn't ask her how to make it because she lived in a town far away. So, I just tried to remember how she made it. It took me all day. When the soup was finally finished, my husband and I sat down to eat it. It tasted terrible! I felt humiliated, and I began to cry. My husband said, "It's all right. It doesn't matter." I knew that he was trying to make me feel better, but he couldn't.

The next day I went to the library in our town. I asked the librarian to give me an easy cookbook. That night I chose a recipe to make for dinner. I followed the directions carefully. My husband said that he liked the meal a lot. I felt more confident. After a few weeks, I went back to the library to get another book. On a trip to Rome with my husband, I went to a store and bought a cookbook with fancy recipes. I tried some of them and they were good. Soon we started to invite friends to dinner. They always enjoyed the meals I made.

I feel proud of myself because I taught myself how to cook. Now I can cook anything I want to.

## THINKING ABOUT THE STORY

1. Do you like this story? Why or why not? Answer in two or three sentences.

    I like/don't like this story because

    _____
    _____
    _____.

2. List any words or expressions from the story that are new to you. Find out what they mean and write the meanings in English or in your native language. Also write the part of speech.

    | Word or Expression | Meaning | Part of Speech |
    |---|---|---|
    | _____ | _____ | _____ |
    | _____ | _____ | _____ |
    | _____ | _____ | _____ |

3. Did you ever teach yourself how to do something? How did it make you feel?

    I taught myself how to _____.

    It made me feel _____
    _____.

4. The writer of this story learned how to cook by starting with an easy cookbook and following the directions carefully. Finish these sentences about yourself, using the example as a guide.

    > **Example:**
    >
    > I learned how to *cook* by *starting with an easy cookbook and following the directions carefully.*

    I learned how to _____ by _____
    _____.

    I learned how to _____ by _____
    _____.

35

### FOCUS: DIRECT AND REPORTED SPEECH

When telling a story, we sometimes like to recall what people said to each other. There are two ways of doing this: through direct speech and through reported speech. In direct speech, we repeat exactly what the people said to each other, putting these words in quotation marks. Here are examples from the first story in this lesson.

He asked me, "Why are you afraid of the water?"
He said, "I'll teach you how to swim."

In reported speech, we report what was said without using the exact words. Here are examples from the second story in the lesson.

I asked the librarian to give me an easy cookbook.
My husband said that he liked the meal a lot.

### Direct Speech

Look closely at the following examples. The important elements are marked.

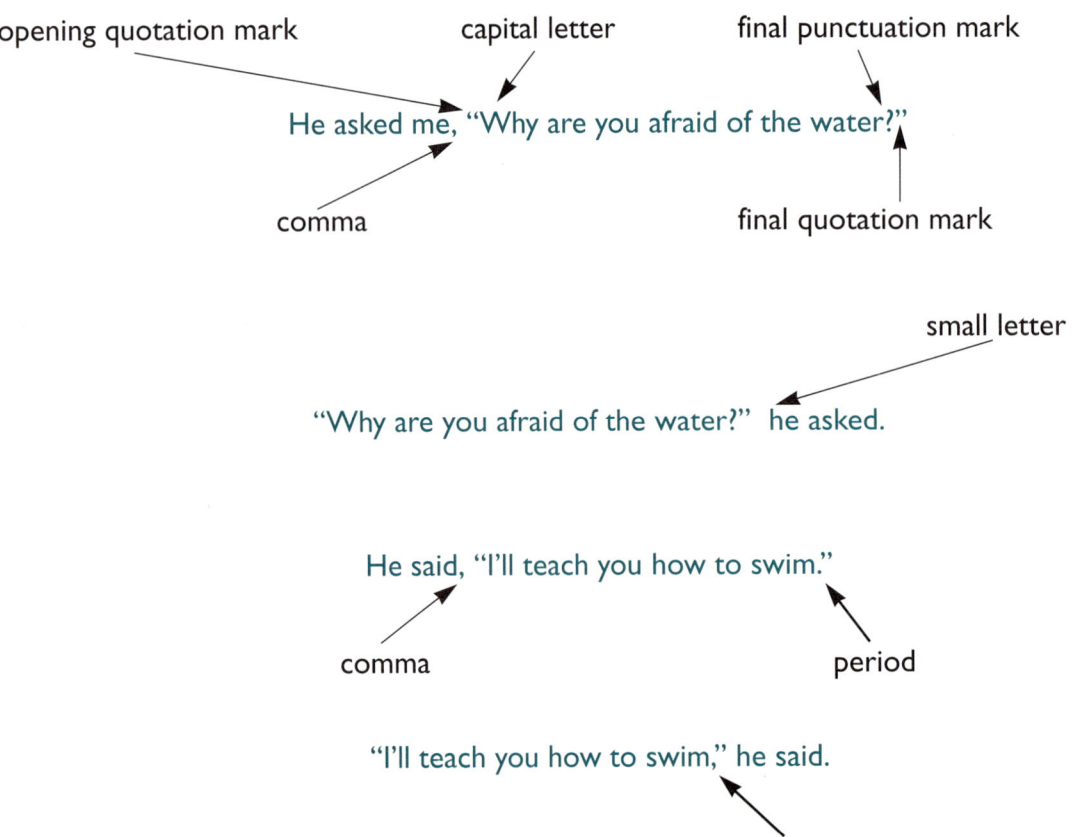

The words most commonly used to describe people talking are *say*, *tell*, *ask*, *answer*, and *reply*.

# Reported Speech

The following chart shows the rules that are applied when direct speech is changed to reported speech.

## Rules for Changing Direct Speech to Reported Speech

| DIRECT SPEECH | REPORTED SPEECH | RULES |
|---|---|---|
| **Statements** | | |
| He said, "I will teach you how to swim." | He said that he would teach me how to swim. | Change personal pronouns. Add that. |
| He said, "It's all right. It doesn't matter." | He said that it was all right and that it didn't matter. | Change present auxiliaries to past. |
| She said, "I jog every morning." | She said that she jogged every morning. | Change present verbs to past. |
| **Yes/No Questions with DO and DID** | | |
| She asked him, "Do you want to dance?" | She asked him if he wanted to dance. | Remove do or did. Add if. Change present verbs to past. |
| **Yes/No Questions with Other Auxiliaries** | | |
| He asked me, "Are you tired?" | He asked me if I was tired. | Add if. Change order of subject and auxiliary. |
| **Information Questions with DO and DID** | | |
| He asked Joan, "Where do you go to college?" | He asked Joan where she went to college. | Remove do or did. Change present verb to past. |
| **Information Questions with Other Auxiliaries** | | |
| He asked Joe, "Where are you going?" | He asked Joe where he was going. | Change order of subject and auxiliary. |
| **Positive Commands** | | |
| "Eat slowly," he said to me. | He told me to eat slowly. | Use told + person spoken to + infinitive verb. |
| **Negative Commands** | | |
| Mary said to her son, "Don't drop out of school." | Mary told her son not to drop out of school. | Use not before infinitive verb. |

For more information about personal pronouns and auxiliaries, see Appendix 2, *Supplementary Material,* pages 120-123.

Finally, when you change direct speech to reported speech, if the events referred to are already over, it is necessary to shift time expressions to the past. For example, in the sentence *He said, "I'll see you tomorrow",* if *tomorrow* has already passed at the time the conversation is reported, the correct version in reported speech is *He said that he would see me the next day.* Here are several time expressions and their corresponding forms in reported speech.

| Direct Speech | Reported Speech |
|---|---|
| yesterday | the day before *or* the previous day |
| today | that day |
| this morning | that morning |
| tomorrow | the next day |
| next week | the following week |

**Exercise.** Read the following conversation, which is written in dialogue form. The two speakers are college students who were having lunch in the cafeteria last month. All the events referred to in the conversation have already occurred. Chin is a male student and Olga is a female student. Rewrite the conversation in paragraph form, first in direct speech and then in reported speech.

Chin: I have an algebra test next week. I'm worried. I think it will be difficult.
Olga: Don't worry about it. You're smart in algebra, and Mr. Thomas is a fair professor.
Chin: What did you get on your English composition?
Olga: The professor gave me a B+. I'm happy about that because I worked hard on it.
Chin: Are you going home now?
Olga: No, I have another class.
Chin: Well, good-bye. Have a good time in class.

### Direct Speech

*Chin said to Olga, "I have an algebra test next week. I think it will be difficult."*

## Reported Speech

*Chin told Olga that he had an algebra test the following week. He thought it would be difficult.*

39

## PULLING IT TOGETHER

1. Do the following exercises in a group of three or four students.

    a. Read "Swimming Lessons" and "Teaching Myself to Cook" in your group. One student will read the first story and another student will read the second story. As you listen to your classmates read, write down any words that you think are mispronounced. Discuss these words after each classmate has finished reading.

    b. Discuss these questions together and then write your answers on the lines provided.

    **"Swimming Lessons"**

    1) How did the writer feel about not being able to swim?

    _____
    _____

    2) Why didn't he want his uncle to teach him to swim at the beach?

    _____
    _____

    3) Do you think that it was a good idea for his uncle to take him to a swimming pool? Why?

    _____
    _____

    **"Teaching Myself to Cook"**

    1) Why do you think the writer decided to make the fish soup the first time she cooked for her husband? Do you think that was a good idea?

    _____
    _____
    _____
    _____

    2) What do you think she realized after she failed to make the fish soup properly?

    _____
    _____
    _____

3) How did the writer feel when she learned how to cook? Why did she feel that way?

_____

_____

_____

c. Tell the members of your group about how you learned to do something. Use the questions below as a guide, and write down notes on the lines provided.

1) How did you feel about not knowing how to _____ ? Why?

_____

_____

_____

2) What made you decide to learn how to _____ ?

_____

_____

_____

3) Did you teach yourself or did someone else teach you?

_____

_____

_____

4) If someone taught you, do you think he or she was a good teacher? Why?

_____

_____

_____

5) How long did it take you to learn? Was it easy or difficult?

_____

_____

_____

6) What, specifically, did you have to do in the process of learning?

_____
_____
_____

7) How did you feel when you finally learned how to _____ ?

_____
_____
_____

2. Now write your own story, using the notes you took above. Write as many drafts as necessary. With your teacher, decide which areas in Appendix 1, *Revising Guidelines,* you should concentrate on at each step in writing your story. You may revise your paper alone or with the help of one or two classmates, according to your teacher's instructions.

3. When you have written your final draft, get together with your group and read your story aloud. Listen to questions or suggestions from your classmates. Make any final changes that you think are necessary.

# CHAPTER
## THREE

# Midsemester Progress Report

*What Am I Doing Right?  What Am I Doing Wrong?*

*Getting Better Every Day*

### What Am I Doing Right? What Am I Doing Wrong?

I am a student at a small college in Chicago. It is now the middle of the semester. Last week I took my ESL class midterm. I don't think I did very well. I am not happy with the progress I'm making in this course.

I like my ESL class a lot. The teacher is very good. He explains things very clearly and he gives us a lot of practice in English. I come to class every day, except when I am sick or I have a problem with my children. I do all the homework and I do all the exercises in class. However, when we have a composition test, I always get a failing grade. I look at my errors and I understand them, but I just make the same errors again the next time we have to write.

I like my classmates and we have fun in class. However, I don't like to speak English to my class. I think they might laugh at me if I make a mistake. Many of my classmates are from my country, and it is easier for me to speak to them in my native language. The teacher gets angry when I do this. He says we have to practice speaking English to each other. I don't like this idea because it makes me feel uncomfortable.

The only time I ever speak English is in my ESL class. In my other classes, mathematics and chemistry, I don't have to speak very much. I just listen to the teacher during class. The tests in these classes don't require a lot of English because we answer the questions with numbers and scientific symbols instead of words. I hear the American students in the college speaking English, but I don't speak to them very often. At home we all speak in my native language. When my children hear me speak English, they laugh at me and tell me I sound funny. They speak English well because they learned it in school.

I don't want to repeat this course, but I think I will have to. I feel very frustrated about my English right now.

*(This composition was written by Anna.)*

### THINKING ABOUT THE STORY

1. Think about how you use English at school and in your personal life. In what ways do you think you are similar to Anna?

2. In what ways are you different from Anna?

3. Share your answers with a classmate.

## Getting Better Every Day

I'm a college student in Washington, D.C. I'm taking an intermediate-level ESL course. It's now the middle of the semester. I think I'm doing well in this course and I'm happy with my progress.

We have a very good teacher. We do a lot of reading, writing, listening, and speaking in class, and we're learning a lot. But our teacher also told us something very important. No one can learn a language well just by coming to class every day. We have to use English in our daily lives outside of class. In this way, English becomes more natural to us.

Some students like to watch television in English. I think this is helpful, but only in a limited way because you don't have to respond to what the people are saying on the television show. I like to practice my English in more active ways. I have conversations with the Americans in my neighborhood. I am looking for a part-time job in an office where everyone speaks English. When I get together with some of my school friends, we often decide to spend a half hour speaking to each other in English. Sometimes we help each other read the local newspaper and discuss the articles in English.

At school, I'm taking a history course and a biology course in English. I feel more confident now about talking to my American professors in English. I just finished writing a research paper in English for my history professor. It wasn't easy, but I got a lot of help from the college librarian and the tutors at the writing center. I'm proud of the steps I am taking to learn English. Every day, English is becoming more and more natural to me.

*(This composition was written by Christina.)*

## THINKING ABOUT THE STORY

1. What do you think of Christina's ideas about learning English? Write your opinion on these lines.

   _____
   _____
   _____

2. Christina writes about several ways to practice English outside of the classroom. Have you ever tried any of these activities? What happened? Write about your experiences on these lines.

   _____
   _____
   _____
   _____

3. Look back to page 7, question number 6 in Chapter 1. This question, given at the beginning of the semester, asked you to make a list of ways to practice English. Have you tried any of these activities? If not, why not? If you have, which activities have helped you? Which activities have not helped you? Write your answers on these lines.

   _____
   _____
   _____
   _____
   _____
   _____

4. How much do you make English a part of your life? In general, do you think you are more like Anna or Christina? Why? Complete the following sentence.

   I am more like _____ because _____
   _____
   _____.

5. Share your answers to these questions with your classmates.

## PULLING IT TOGETHER

The following activities are designed to encourage you to express how you feel about learning English. They should help you to think about where you are right now in your process of learning English. They should also help you to incorporate English more fully into your life.

### In-Class Writing Activities

1. Write a letter to your ESL teacher, expressing how you feel about the class. Tell the teacher how well you think you are doing in the class and how you feel about the progress you are making.

2. Write a letter to Anna, giving her advice about how she can progress more in learning English.

### Out-of-Class Projects and Writing Assignments

1. Interview another student in the class. Find out what the student thinks about the class. Then find out how the student is progressing. Finally, ask the student what things he or she does outside of class to practice English. Write a composition about this student's feelings and experiences and compare them with your own feelings about and experiences with English.

2. With one or two other students, tape-record a discussion on a topic that is interesting to all of you. The rules are that everyone must speak only English, and the discussion must last at least thirty minutes. When the discussion ends, listen to the tape and talk about what happened. Then, each student will write a composition about the experience.

3. Interview a person who is learning English as a second language and who has to speak English at work. Find out how the person felt when he or she started working. Also find out how the person deals with the problems of communicating in English. Finally, ask what impact working at that job has had on his or her process of learning English. Write a composition about what you learn.

4. Make friends with an American at your college or in your neighborhood. The person should be someone who doesn't speak your native language. Write a composition about your friend and about your experiences speaking to him or her.

5. Decide to spend one day speaking only English. You can tell your family and friends what you are planning to do before the day arrives. Write a composition describing what happens.

# CHAPTER FOUR

# Influences on My Life

**Lesson 1:** A Person Who Has Influenced Me

*A Model Woman*

*A Different Kind of Father*

Focus: *It + Be + Adjective*

**Lesson 2:** An Event That Has Influenced Me

*Losing a Friend to Drugs*

*A Story of Prejudice*

Focus: The Present Perfect and Past Perfect Tenses

# LESSON ONE: A Person Who Has Influenced Me

### A Model Woman

My Aunt Maria is a person who has influenced my life a great deal. She is a model for me as a woman and a mother.

Aunt Maria was married in a small town in Oaxaca, Mexico, when she was eighteen. She was very content in her marriage. She and her husband had four children. Everything went well for eight years. Then one day, her husband had a heart attack and died. No one expected that to happen because he was still very young. Aunt Maria was in a bad situation. She didn't have any money to raise her children and her family couldn't help her. She felt desperate.

Then, she decided to move her family to Mexico City because she thought it would be easier to find a job there. Even though she had been a homemaker all her life, she managed to get a job in a law office. Her children were doing well and they were happy. However, after a few years Aunt Maria became bored. She made another decision: to go to law school. She wanted to become a lawyer to help people with their problems.

Even though Aunt Maria was thirty years old, she went to college and to law school. While she was studying, she also worked and took care of all her children. When she became a lawyer, her family was very proud of her. Now she helps divorced and widowed women with their legal and economic problems.

Aunt Maria is a model for me. I learned from her story that at anytime in my life, I can improve my situation by making a change in my life. It takes a lot of courage to do that. However, when I feel scared about doing something new, I remember Aunt Maria and my courage returns.

**THINKING ABOUT THE STORY**

1. Write your reactions to this story in a few sentences.

   _____
   _____
   _____
   _____

2. List any words or expressions from the story that are new to you. Find out what they mean and write the meanings in English or in your native language. Also write the part of speech.

   | Word or Expression | Meaning | Part of Speech |
   | --- | --- | --- |
   |  |  |  |
   |  |  |  |
   |  |  |  |
   |  |  |  |

3. Finish these sentences about the story.

   a. Aunt Maria's husband died of a heart attack even though _____
   _____.

   b. Even though Aunt Maria had always been a homemaker, _____
   _____.

   c. Even though Aunt Maria was thirty years old, _____
   _____.

4. What do you think were the reasons Aunt Maria wanted to become a lawyer? Write your ideas on these lines.

   _____
   _____
   _____
   _____
   _____

### A Different Kind of Father

When I was a boy I always knew that when I grew up, I would get married and have children. My marriage would be like my parents' marriage: I would work and my wife would take care of the children. However, my ideas changed when my cousin George got married and started a family of his own eight years ago.

George's mother died when he was a baby, and his father took care of him and his sisters when they were young. So George wanted to do the same thing for his children. When his wife Fatima had their first baby, a boy, George learned how to feed him and change him. On weekends, when George didn't work, Fatima could go shopping or visiting while George took care of the baby. He enjoyed doing this even though other people thought it was strange.

Now, George and Fatima's son is seven and they also have a five-year-old girl. Three days a week, George comes home from work early so that Fatima can go to her college classes. George takes the children to the park where they can play. If one of the children gets hurt, George knows what to do. If his son starts to fight with another child, George disciplines him. George enjoys taking care of his children. He thinks that the time he spends with them makes them feel close to their father. Both George and Fatima feel that their whole family is closer because both of them take care of the children.

Many people think that only a mother can take care of her children. However, George's example makes me think differently. I believe now that a father has the same ability to take care of children as a mother. When I have a family, I want to take care of my children like George does. I will get satisfaction from doing this and my family will be very close.

**THINKING ABOUT THE STORY**

1. Write your reaction to this story in a few sentences.

   _____
   _____
   _____
   _____
   _____
   _____

2. List any words or expressions from the story that are new to you. Find out what they mean and write the meanings in English or in your native language. Also, write the part of speech.

   | Word or Expression | Meaning | Part of Speech |
   |---|---|---|
   | _____ | _____ | _____ |
   | _____ | _____ | _____ |
   | _____ | _____ | _____ |
   | _____ | _____ | _____ |
   | _____ | _____ | _____ |
   | _____ | _____ | _____ |

3. The writer of this story had certain ideas about marriage when he was younger. When you were younger, were your ideas about marriage the same as his ideas or different from his ideas? Look at the sentence below. Cross out *the same as* or *different from* and add one or two sentences, giving your explanation.

   When I was younger, my ideas about marriage were the same as/different from the writer's ideas. _____

   _____
   _____
   _____
   _____
   _____

4. The writer's ideas about marriage changed because of the example of his cousin George. Today, are your ideas about marriage the same as or different from what they were when you were younger? Cross out *the same as* or *different from* in the sentence below. Add a few more sentences to explain your ideas.

My ideas about marriage today are the same as/different from the ideas I had when I was younger. _____

_____
_____
_____
_____
_____
_____
_____
_____
_____
_____
_____
_____

5. Discuss your answers to numbers 3 and 4 with a classmate.

## FOCUS: *IT* + *BE* + ADJECTIVE

In some languages, it is not necessary for every sentence to have a subject. In English, however, a subject is always necessary. In one type of sentence, the word *it* takes the place of a subject when there is no other word to put there. The word *it* in this case is sometimes called an "empty subject." It is followed by a conjugation of the verb *be* and an adjective or an adjective phrase. Here are two examples of this sentence type in the stories you have just read.

> She thought *it would be easier* to find a job there.
> People thought *it was strange*.

*Would be* and *was* are both forms of the verb *be*. *Easier* and *strange* are adjectives.

This type of expression can be used several ways. The three basic parts — *it* + *be* + *adjective* — can stand alone, as in the following sentence.

> *It is surprising* that John didn't come to the party.

One variation is to add an *infinitive verb* at the end, as in this sentence.

> I didn't know that *it was so difficult to write* a history paper.

Another variation is to add *for* + *a reference to a person* + *an infinitive verb*. Here are two examples.

> I think that *it will be interesting for my daughter to learn* about different cultures.
> *It is difficult for me to study and work* at the same time.

This expression can be used in the negative as well as in the positive. Look at these examples.

> It *isn't* very important for me to know how to type.
> I knew that it *would not be* easy to find an apartment.
> It *won't be* necessary for you to bring anything when you come to my house for dinner.

**Exercise.** Use the word *it* plus words and expressions from the following three lists to write your own sentences. Use the words and expressions in any combination you wish.

| | | |
|---|---|---|
| is/isn't | exciting | for me |
| was/wasn't | entertaining | for me and my family |
| will/won't be | fascinating | for my son/daughter/mother/ |
| can/can't be | useful | father/wife/husband |
| should/shouldn't be | frightening | for me and my friend/friends |
| could/couldn't be | boring | for me and my classmates |
| would/wouldn't be | educational | for (name of a person) |
| | important | |
| | necessary | |

> **Examples:**
> It is educational for me to watch the evening news.
> It should be easy for my son to adjust to life in the United States.

1. _____

2. _____

3. _____

4. _____

5. _____

6. _____

**PULLING IT TOGETHER**

1. Do the following exercises in a group of three or four students.

   a. Read "A Model Woman" and "A Different Kind of Father" in your group. One student will read the first story aloud and another student will read the second story. As you listen to your classmates read, write down any words that you think are mispronounced. Discuss these words after each classmate has finished reading.

   b. Discuss the following questions as a group, and then write your answers on the lines provided.

      1) Do you see any similarities between Maria and George in their life situations and in their personalities?

      _____
      _____
      _____
      _____
      _____
      _____
      _____
      _____
      _____
      _____

      2) Do you think people of your culture would approve or disapprove of the way Maria or George decided to live their lives? Why?

      _____
      _____
      _____
      _____
      _____
      _____
      _____
      _____
      _____

c. Think of a person who has influenced your life in some way, a person who is a model for you. It can be someone you know personally or someone famous that you admire. Tell your group about this person. Using the questions below as a guide, write your answers on the lines provided.

   1) How and when did you first meet or learn about this person?

   _____
   _____
   _____

   2) What characteristics of this person do you admire?

   _____
   _____
   _____

   3) What does (or did) this person do that makes you admire him or her?

   _____
   _____
   _____

   4) How has this person influenced your life?

   _____
   _____
   _____

2. Now write your own story about a person who has influenced you in your life. Choose someone who is a model for you. Write as many drafts as necessary. With your teacher, decide which areas in Appendix 1, *Revising Guidelines,* you should concentrate on at each step in writing your story. You may revise your paper alone or with the help of one or two classmates, according to your teacher's instructions.

3. When you have written your final draft, get together with your group and read your story aloud. Listen to questions or suggestions from your classmates. Make any final changes that you think are necessary.

# LESSON TWO: An Event That Has Influenced Me

## Losing a Friend to Drugs

When I was a teenager, I lived in Chinatown in San Francisco. I had many friends there. My best friend's name was Kwan, but we called him Kenny. What happened to him was very sad and it has influenced me ever since.

Kenny was a good kid. He did well in school and obeyed his parents. However, Kenny's weakness was that he wanted everyone to like him. If someone told him to do something, he did it just to please that person. One day Kenny was invited to a party by some boys from our high school. I knew that these boys took drugs and I warned Kenny not to go, but he went anyway. The next day I asked him how the party was. He didn't say very much about it.

Over the next few weeks, I noticed that Kenny started to change. He looked sloppy, he spoke very little, and he stopped doing his school work. One day I asked him directly if he was taking drugs. He said that he was, and that the drugs made him feel good. I tried to tell him to stop, but he wouldn't listen to me. That night I went to Kenny's house. I told his mother that Kenny was taking drugs. She didn't believe me. She insisted that her son was a good boy. I felt terrible and frustrated because I couldn't help my friend.

One week passed. On Saturday night I got a phone call from Kenny's brother. Kenny was in the hospital. When I got to the hospital, he was already dead. The doctor said that he had taken some cocaine that was bad. There was not enough time for the doctor to save him.

I miss Kenny very much, but his death taught me a lot. I learned that you can't be friends with everyone, and you have to choose your friends very carefully. I also learned that drugs are bad. When I have children, I will tell them all the time to stay away from drugs. These were very painful lessons for me because they came with the death of my best friend.

### THINKING ABOUT THE STORY

1. In a few sentences, write about your reaction to this story.

   _____
   _____
   _____
   _____
   _____

2. List any words or expressions from the story that are new to you. Find out what they mean and write the meanings in English or in your native language. Also write the part of speech.

   **Word or Expression**    **Meaning**                                **Part of Speech**

   _____    _____    _____
   _____    _____    _____
   _____    _____    _____

3. In the story, the writer tried to give advice to his friend Kenny. How do you think Kenny reacted to this advice, and why did he react that way? Write your answer on these lines.

   _____
   _____
   _____
   _____
   _____

4. Choose either *(a)* or *(b)*. Write your answer on the lines provided.

   a. Was there a time in your life when you tried to give someone advice? How did that person feel? How did you feel? Describe what happened.

   b. Was there a time in your life when someone tried to give you advice? How did you feel? How did the other person feel? Describe what happened.

   _____
   _____
   _____
   _____
   _____
   _____
   _____
   _____
   _____
   _____
   _____
   _____
   _____
   _____
   _____
   _____
   _____
   _____
   _____
   _____

5. Share your answers to numbers 3 and 4 with one or two classmates.

## A Story of Prejudice

When I first came to this country, I had a job making jewelry in a factory. I worked next to Yvonne, an American girl who is black. We became friends, and she told me a story about her family that taught me something about prejudice in this country.

Yvonne lived with her family in Philadelphia. The family was very big and lived in a small apartment. Yvonne's father worked hard and saved enough money to buy a house. They were happy in the house, but there was a problem. Most of the houses in that neighborhood belonged to white families. The while families didn't want Yvonne's family to live there. Her family started to get strange phone calls in the middle of the night. White children called out bad names to Yvonne and her brothers and sisters when they walked to school in the morning or came home in the afternoon. No one talked to Yvonne's mother when she went shopping at the supermarket. Everyone in her family felt terrible, but they couldn't move again because all their money was spent on their new house.

One weekend, Yvonne and her family went to visit relatives in Boston. When they returned Sunday night, they had a big shock. Their house had burned down. They lost all their possessions, but they thanked God that no one was hurt. With the insurance money that they got after the fire, the family moved to another house in a black neighborhood. The police never found out who was responsible for the fire, but everyone guessed that it was started by some of the white people in the neighborhood.

I was very surprised when I heard this story. I knew that many Americans don't like immigrants from other countries, but I didn't know that many white Americans hate other Americans because they are black. I believe that everyone should fight against prejudice whenever it happens. This is what I will try to do in my life because we are all the children of God.

### THINKING ABOUT THE STORY

1. When you read this story, did you react to what happened to Yvonne's family in the same way that the writer did? In other words, were you surprised by her story? Explain your answer on these lines.

2. List any words or expressions from the story that are new to you. Find out what they mean and write the meanings in English or in your native language. Also write the part of speech.

   **Word or Expression**     **Meaning**     **Part of Speech**

3. How would you define the word *prejudice*? Why do you think people are prejudiced?

4. Some people think that prejudice exists in all groups of people (white, black, Hispanic, Chinese, and so forth). Think about the people in your native country. Does prejudice exist among them? If it does, what kinds of things do the prejudiced people say or do to show their prejudice? Write your ideas on these lines.

_____
_____
_____
_____
_____
_____
_____
_____
_____
_____
_____
_____
_____
_____
_____
_____
_____
_____
_____
_____

5. Share your answers to numbers 3 and 4 with one or two classmates.

## FOCUS: THE PRESENT PERFECT AND PAST PERFECT TENSES

Here are examples of the present perfect tense from this lesson and from a previous lesson.

What happened to him was very sad and it *has influenced* me ever since.
My Aunt Maria is a person who *has influenced* my life a great deal.

Here are examples from the stories of the past perfect tense.

The doctor said that he *had taken* some cocaine that was bad.
When they returned Sunday night, they had a big shock. Their house *had burned* down.

### The Present Perfect

This tense is formed with the word *has* or *have* + *the past participle*. For regular verbs, the past participle is the same as the simple past tense. The past participles of many irregular verbs are listed in Appendix 2, *Supplementary Material*, on 124-125.

Use the present perfect when you are referring to an activity or state of mind that began in the past and continues in the present. The following time line illustrates the use of the present perfect in the first example sentence above.

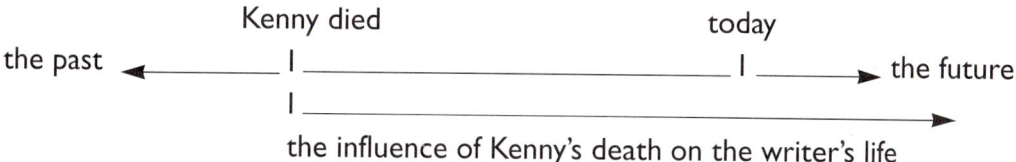

At the time of Kenny's death, the writer learned something, and his way of thinking changed. This way of thinking continues in the present, and probably will continue into the future. Also, notice the difference between the use of the simple past tense and the present perfect. Kenny *died* on a specific day; his death is now an event in the past. However, the fact of his death continues to influence the writer; therefore, Kenny's death *has influenced* the writer ever since.

Two expressions that are often used with the present perfect are *since (a certain date or period)* and *for (a certain length of time)*. Look at these two ways of expressing the idea stated below in parentheses. Then look at the time line, which illustrates the idea.

(I arrived in the United States in 1985. It is now 1992.)
 I *have lived* in the United States *since 1985*.
 I *have lived* in the United States *for seven years*.

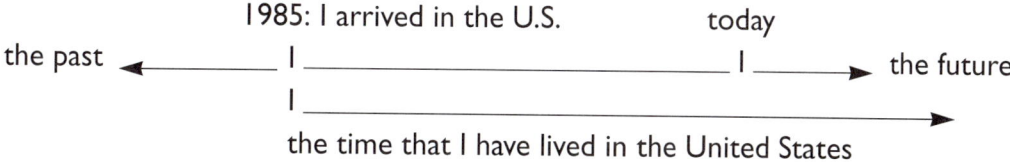

The present perfect is also used to describe an activity that has happened a number of times, repeatedly, since a certain time in the past. You can use *since (a certain date or period)* and *in the last (a certain period of time)* to express that idea. Here are some examples.

*Since last July,* I have gone to the movies five times.
I have visited Disney World many times *since I was a child.*
*In the last two years,* Mark has gone to three weddings.

The present perfect can also be used to describe something that has always or has never been true in a person's life. (In the following examples, notice the position of the words *always* and *never*. Frequency adverbs like these are always placed between *have* and the past participle.)

I *have always wanted* to be a doctor.
I *have never eaten* Indonesian food.

## The Past Perfect

The past perfect is formed with the word *had + the past participle*. This tense is used to describe an activity or state of mind that began at a time in the past and continued until another point in the past. At the time that the speaker or writer tells of the activity, it is already finished. Study these examples with their time lines.

I *got* a job at a gas station in 1983. I *had worked* there for three years when the station closed down and I *lost* my job.

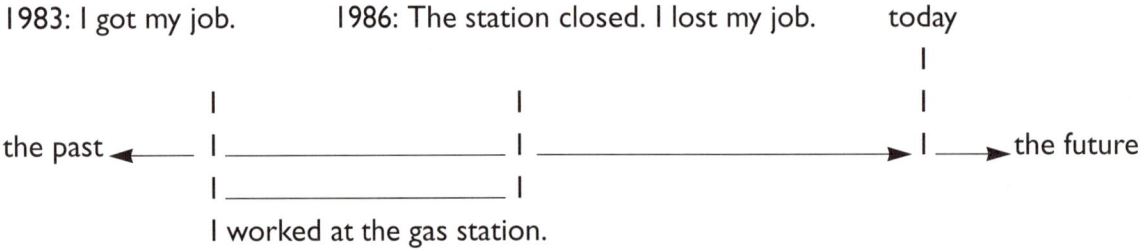

Before I *went* to Africa, I *had always dreamed* of going there to see the wild animals. In 1975, I went to Africa and realized my dream.

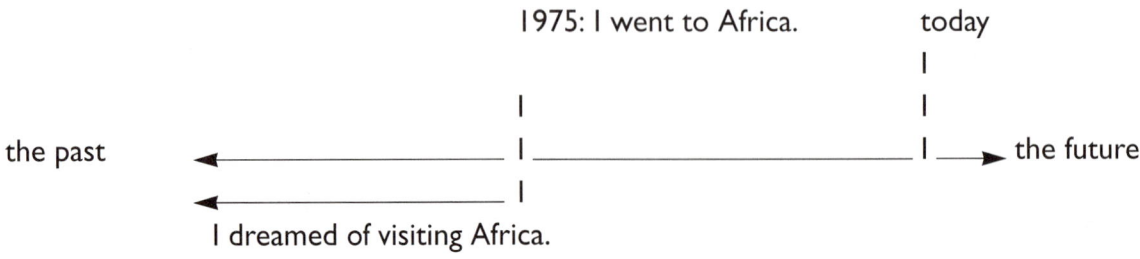

Two examples from the stories illustrate another use of the past perfect. In these sentences, two events that happened at different times in the past are mentioned. The earlier event is looked back on from the perspective of the more recent event.

The doctor said that he [Kenny] *had taken* some cocaine that was bad.

```
              Kenny took the bad cocaine.              today
the past ←——— | ————————————————— | ————————————— | ———→ the future
                                   |
                    The doctor said that Kenny had taken some bad cocaine.
```

(Note that the sentence above is an example of reported speech, which was discussed in Chapter 2, Lesson 2.)

When they returned Sunday night, they had a big shock. Their house *had burned* down.

```
              Their house burned down.                 today
the past ←——— | ————————————————— | ————————————— | ———→ the future
                                   |
                  They returned home and saw that their house had burned down.
```

**Exercise 1.** Complete these sentences by using the correct form of the verbs in parentheses. Choose the present perfect, the past perfect, or the simple past tense. The time expressions should help you decide which tense to use. Remember to place frequency adverbs between *have* or *had* and the past participle.

> **Example:**
> Since I *left* my country three years ago, I have *written* many letters to my friends and
>     (leave)                                  (write)
> relatives there.

1. I _____ married on June 5, 1965. Since that day, I _____ very happy.
   (get)                                                    (be)

2. Jane _____ in that house for four years. She still enjoys living there.
        (live)

67

3. Last night, when Jim _____ (arrive) at the party, he _____ (discover) that his friends _____ (eat) the entire birthday cake.

4. When I arrived in this city, I _____ (find) an apartment that was not too expensive. At the time the landlord _____ (decide) to raise the rent, I _____ (live) there for five years.

5. Since she _____ (start) college last September, Martha _____ (make) many new friends.

6. Until he _____ (go) to Japan last month, George _____ (eat - never) Japanese food.

7. Margaret _____ (have) her first baby in 1982. Since that time, she _____ (have) three more children.

8. I _____ (meet) Philip three months ago. Since then, he _____ (invite) me to his home five times.

9. Yesterday, Amy _____ (tell) me to meet her at her house at 6:00 P.M., but when I _____ (get) there, she _____ (leave - already).

10. When I _____ (visit) London five years ago, I _____ (see) a famous old theater. However, when I _____ (return) to London last year, I was disappointed to see that they _____ (destroy) the theater in order to build a new one in its place.

**Exercise 2.** Choose five sentences from Exercise 1 and rewrite them, using information relating to your own life.

> **Example (from number 5)**
> 
> Since I started college last year, I have learned many new things.

1. _____
_____

2. 

3. 

4. 

5. 

**PULLING IT TOGETHER**

1. Do the following exercises in a group of three or four students.

   a. Read "Losing a Friend to Drugs" and "A Story of Prejudice" in your group. One student will read the first story aloud and another student will read the second story. As you listen to your classmates read, write down any words that you think are mispronounced. Discuss these words after each classmate has finished reading.

   b. These stories deal with two serious problems today: drugs and prejudice. Has one of these problems affected you personally since you came to this country? Talk about it with the members of your group and then write your answer on the lines below.

c. In these stories, the writers were influenced by or learned from something that happened *to someone else*. Think of something that happened to another person that has influenced you. The person might be someone you know personally, like a relative or a friend. The person might also be someone you read about in a book or in a magazine, or someone you heard about on television. Tell the other group members who the person is, what happened to him or her, and how this event influenced your own life. Try to remember as many details as you can. Use the lines below for notes.

The person: _____

What happened to him or her: _____

_____

_____

_____

_____

_____

_____

_____

_____

How it influenced me: _____

_____

_____

_____

_____

_____

2. Now write your story about an event that happened to someone else that influenced you. Write as many drafts as necessary. With your teacher, decide which areas in Appendix 1, *Revising Guidelines,* you should concentrate on at each step in writing your story. You may revise your paper alone or with the help of one or two classmates, according to your teacher's instructions.

3. When you have written your final draft, get together with your group and read your story aloud. Listen to questions or suggestions from your classmates. Make any final changes you think are necessary.

# CHAPTER FIVE

# Imagining

**Lesson 1:** In My Favorite Place

*Central Park*

*In My Backyard*

Focus: *There + Be + Noun*

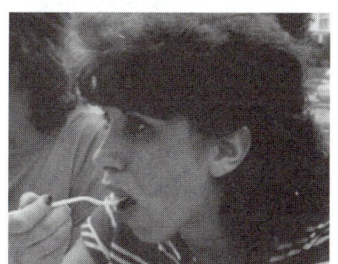

**Lesson 2:** Change of Identity

*Rock Star*

*Mayor*

Focus: Gerund and Infinitive Phrases

# LESSON ONE: In My Favorite Place

## Central Park

I am standing in my favorite spot in Central Park. It is on a hill with many trees. There are a few people sitting near me, but it's not too crowded.

It is a weekday afternoon in January. It's a beautiful day. The sun is shining and the air is crisp, not biting cold like it is on many winter days. From this hill, I can see many things. Far away I see the skyline of Manhattan. The buildings are so clear that even the windows are visible. The buildings look clean and elegant from this view although close up they are ugly and dirty. I wonder how many people it took to make those fancy buildings. I wonder about the people who work inside them. There are so many people going to those buildings in the morning, going home at night to so many families. New York is such a large city. Sometimes it is hard for me to imagine how many people live here.

When I look down from the hill, I see a skating rink. It is busy and gleaming. Sometimes a couple skates by holding hands. Maybe they are in love and talking about getting married. I enjoy watching the couples skating by gracefully. I listen to the birds in the trees nearby, making funny noises as they talk to each other. I see the sun slowly getting lower in the sky. Soon I start to feel cool and I know it's time to go home.

I like to go to this spot in the park after work. When I am here, I stop thinking about everything in my life: my job, my family, my studies. For about an hour, I just stand and watch all the wonders of the world around me. I just appreciate everything that God put on this earth for us to enjoy.

### THINKING ABOUT THE STORY

1. Write your reaction to this story in a few sentences.

   _____
   _____
   _____
   _____
   _____
   _____
   _____

2. List any words or expressions from the story that are new to you. Find out what they mean and write the meanings in English or in your native language. Also write the part of speech.

   | Word or Expression | Meaning | Part of Speech |
   | --- | --- | --- |
   |  |  |  |
   |  |  |  |
   |  |  |  |
   |  |  |  |
   |  |  |  |
   |  |  |  |
   |  |  |  |
   |  |  |  |
   |  |  |  |

3. The writer describes the view from a favorite spot in the park. For example, the writer says, *I see the skyline of Manhattan,* and *I see the sun slowly getting lower.* Pretend you are in a park that is familiar to you. Describe what you see.

   a. I see _____
   _____
   _____ .

   b. I see _____
   _____
   _____ .

   c. I see _____
   _____
   _____ .

   d. I see _____
   _____
   _____ .

4. The writer seems to enjoy having some time alone for thinking about special things. Do you enjoy being alone sometimes? Why or why not? What do you think about when you are alone? Write your thoughts here.

   _____
   _____
   _____
   _____
   _____
   _____
   _____
   _____
   _____
   _____

5. Share your answers to numbers 3 and 4 with one or two classmates.

## In My Backyard

It is Sunday afternoon and I am in the backyard of my house in Santo Domingo. The backyard is a large square with grass and some trees around it. It is not very fancy, but it is the place that I enjoy the most.

It is early in the afternoon. Some of my relatives and friends from the neighborhood have come to enjoy a barbecue with me and my family. There are many comfortable chairs for everyone to sit on. The radio is playing the Latin music that we all like, and some of my friends are dancing. I am at the barbecue, preparing the meat for our meal. The smoke comes up into my eyes, but the smell that it makes is very pleasing. My wife is in the kitchen preparing the rest of the meal. We will have rice, chicken, pork, vegetables, and coffee and cake for dessert. My sister brings out some soda for us to drink because it's very hot outside. The soda tastes especially wonderful to me because I am so close to the fire.

Everyone is having a good time. Some people are arguing about politics. My father is getting very excited about something that he read in the paper, as he always does. There are many children chasing each other around the backyard. I see my son playing with them, but my daughter is sitting quietly near the radio. I notice that she is wearing a very pretty dress and she looks very grown up. I realize that she is becoming a young lady and she doesn't want to play with the others, like a child. I am very proud of her.

    Soon we all sit down and have a delicious meal. We talk about everything that is happening in the neighborhood and we tell many jokes. This is my favorite place and my favorite day because I can relax from my week at work and enjoy being with the people I love: my family and my friends.

## THINKING ABOUT THE STORY

1. Write your reaction to this story in a few sentences.

   _____
   _____
   _____
   _____
   _____

2. List any words or expressions from the story that are new to you. Find out what they mean and write the meanings in English or in your native language. Also, write the part of speech.

   | Word or Expression | Meaning | Part of Speech |
   |---|---|---|
   | _____ | _____ | _____ |
   | _____ | _____ | _____ |
   | _____ | _____ | _____ |
   | _____ | _____ | _____ |
   | _____ | _____ | _____ |
   | _____ | _____ | _____ |
   | _____ | _____ | _____ |
   | _____ | _____ | _____ |
   | _____ | _____ | _____ |

3. The writer uses different senses to describe what it is like to be in his favorite place. Write down what he hears, smells, tastes, feels physically, and feels emotionally.

   a. The writer hears _____
   _____.

   b. He smells _____
   _____.

   c. He tastes _____
   _____.

   d. He feels (physically) _____
   _____.

   e. He feels (emotionally) _____
   _____.

4. Pretend that you are in a room in your house or apartment, at a particular time of day. What do you see, hear, smell, taste, feel physically, and feel emotionally? Describe this scene in the paragraph below, using as many senses as possible.

   I am _____.
       (where you are)

   It is _____ . _____
       (the time of day)

   _____
   _____
   _____
   _____
   _____
   _____
   _____
   _____

5. Share your answers to numbers 3 and 4 with one or two classmates.

## FOCUS: *THERE* + *BE* + NOUN

In Chapter 4, Lesson 1, you learned how to use the "empty subject" *it* with the verb *be* and an adjective. Another word which serves as an "empty subject" is the word *there*. However, while *it* is followed by an adjective or an adjective phrase, *there* is followed by a noun or noun phrase. *There* + *be* is used when you want to state that something exists. Look at these examples from the stories in this lesson.

> *There are* so many people, going to all those buildings in the morning, going home at night to so many families.
>
> *There are* many comfortable chairs for everyone to sit on.
>
> *There are* many children chasing each other around the backyard.
>
> Sometimes *it is* hard for me to imagine how many people live here.

Notice that *so many people, many comfortable chairs,* and *many children* are noun phrases; *hard,* following *it,* is an adjective.

Like the expression *it* + *be* + *adjective, there* + *be* + *noun* can be followed by *an infinitive verb* or by *for* + *a reference to a person* + *an infinitive verb.*

> *There was no time to call* before we left.
>
> *There are enough chairs for everyone to sit down.*

*There* + *be* + noun can be used with *be* in any tense you wish, in the singular or plural form, and in the positive or negative. Here are some examples.

> There *will be* many exciting things happening tomorrow.
>
> There *should be* a home for everyone in this country.
>
> There *were* only two apples left in the refrigerator.
>
> There *was* a wonderful movie on television last night.
>
> If you eat all the ice cream now, there *won't* be any left for dessert tonight.

**Exercise 1.** Look around the room you are in right now. Write a paragraph describing what you see, using *there is* or *there are* in at least four sentences.

Right now I am in _____.

_____

_____

_____

_____

_____

_____

_____

_____

_____

_____

**Exercise 2.** Think about a place in your past — for example, the house you lived in, the school you went to, a park you played in, a beach you went to. Write a paragraph describing that place, using *there was* or *there were* in at least four sentences.

I remember _____.

_____

_____

_____

_____

_____

_____

_____

_____

_____

_____

**Exercise 3.** Complete these sentences in any way you wish.

1. I believe that there should be _____

_____

_____

_____

_____.

2. In the future, I hope that there won't be _____

_____

_____

_____

_____.

3. When I started college, I thought that there would be _____

_____

_____

_____

_____.

4. When I started college, I didn't think that there would be _____

_____

_____

_____

_____.

5. My first impression of this country was that there was/were _____

_____

_____

_____

_____.

...................................................................

...ises in a group of three or four students.

...and "In My Backyard" in your group.  One student will read the ...another student will read the second story.  As you listen to your ...e down any words that you think are mispronounced.  Discuss ...h classmate has finished reading.

...here you feel very comfortable.  Discuss the following questions ...write the answers that are best for you and give reasons for your

...refer to be alone or with other people?  If you prefer to be with ...ou prefer to be with a few people or with a large crowd?

_____

_____

_____

_____

2) Do you generally prefer to be indoors or outdoors?

_____

_____

_____

_____

_____

3) Do you like to be in places that are new and unfamiliar to you, or do you like to be in places that you know very well?

_____

_____

_____

_____

_____

c. Now work individually. Think of one place that is very special to you. Pretend that you are there right now, using all your senses to remember what it is like. As you remember, fill in the lines below with as many details as you can. When everyone in your group is finished, share your answers.

Right now I am _____.

I see _____

_____

_____.

I hear _____

_____

_____.

I smell _____

_____

_____.

I taste _____

_____

_____.

I feel _____

_____

_____.

2. Now write your own story, imagining that you are in your favorite place. Use the notes that you made above for ideas. Write as many drafts as necessary. With your teacher, decide which areas in Appendix 1, *Revising Guidelines,* you should concentrate on at each step in writing your story. You may revise your paper alone or with the help of one or two classmates, according to your teacher's instructions.

3. When you have written your final draft, get together with your group and read your story aloud. Listen to questions or suggestions from your classmates. Make any final changes you think are necessary.

# LESSON TWO  Change of Identity

*Writing is a good way to explore your imagination, to let it take you away from where and who you are right now. The authors of the next two stories imagine what it would be like to be someone different, and to lead a very different life from their own.*

## Rock Star

My name is Ricky and I play the drums in a rock and roll band. In the past two years, the band has become popular all over the country. The dream of my life has come true and now I'm a rock star.

My life is very busy. Six months of the year we travel from city to city giving concerts. During these tours, we spend a lot of time on airplanes. Traveling so much can really be tiring. We try to catch up on our sleep during these plane trips, but it's sometimes difficult. When we arrive in a city, we have to begin rehearsing right away. Six nights a week we perform. It's very exciting to see people enjoying our music. We get back to our hotel about 3:00 A.M., and we sleep for about seven hours. Then we have to get up and rehearse for the next performance.

When we're not on tour, we also have a busy schedule. We're always working on new songs. We have made a few albums, which is very hard work because you have to do songs over and over again in the studio until they come out right. In order to increase our popularity, we appear on television shows and at record stores. We also give interviews to newspaper and magazine writers.

This kind of life allows us many wonderful opportunities. We get invited to fancy parties and restaurants all the time. We make enough money to live in beautiful apartments. One of the best things about being a rock star is that we get to meet many beautiful girls. Some girls come to the same concert every night and try to get into our hotel rooms and apartments. But we have to be careful about these girls because some of them can be really crazy.

I love the life that I am leading now. But I am still very young and I think that in four or five years I will become tired of this life. Eventually I would like to get married and have a family. I won't travel so much anymore and I will have a quieter life.

### THINKING ABOUT THE STORY

1. Write your reaction to this story in a few sentences.

   _____
   _____
   _____
   _____

2. List any words or expressions from the story that are new to you. Find out what they mean and write the meanings in English or in your native language. Also write the part of speech.

   | Word or Expression | Meaning | Part of Speech |
   | --- | --- | --- |
   | _____ | _____ | _____ |
   | _____ | _____ | _____ |
   | _____ | _____ | _____ |
   | _____ | _____ | _____ |
   | _____ | _____ | _____ |
   | _____ | _____ | _____ |
   | _____ | _____ | _____ |

3. According to Ricky, what are the advantages of being a rock star?

4. According to Ricky, what are the disadvantages of being a rock star?

5. Would you like to be a rock star? Why or why not?

6. Share your answers to numbers 3, 4, and 5 with your classmates.

*Like Ricky, Cynthia thinks about what it would be to lead a life very different from her own. In this composition, she imagines that she is the mayor of a major city.*

## Mayor

My name is Cynthia and I am the mayor of a large city. I have a very challenging life.

I have worked very hard to get to the position I have now. I went to law school and worked for a large law firm in the city. Then, I decided to go into politics because I saw that there were many problems in the city that were not being solved. I worked at several jobs in the city government before I decided to run for mayor. I had a very difficult campaign, but with the help of my friends and supporters I won the election to the highest position in the city government.

My day is very busy. In the morning I meet with my staff to review my schedule for the day. I often have meetings with citizens' groups who come to complain about problems in their neighborhoods, like drug trafficking, poor police protection, or poorly maintained apartment buildings. I do the best I can to help them, but sometimes they don't realize how complicated it is to run a big city and try to solve all its problems. In the afternoon I go to the meetings of the city council, where we discuss new laws. These meetings often go on for hours and are very tiring. In the evening I often have to attend receptions or neighborhood functions. However, I try to keep a few nights a week free to stay home and relax with my husband and children.

The most difficult part of my career is trying to maintain a private life. When I go out somewhere with my family, there are always photographers and reporters following us. At first, my children liked the attention and thought it was fun. But now they are getting tired of it, and sometimes they say that they wish they had an "ordinary" mother. My husband is very understanding, but he also gets impatient with all the people who follow us.

Despite these problems, I am very glad to have the opportunity to serve my city a mayor. Since I was elected, I have achieved some major accomplishments. I have raised a lot of money to build apartments for low-income families. I have helped set up more treatment centers for people addicted to drugs and alcohol. I started a program in which major corporations hire and train unemployed young people from the poor areas of the city. I have encouraged the opening of more day-care centers so that more mothers can go to work and increase their family incomes. I am proud of these accomplishments and I hope to do a lot more during my term as mayor of this city.

## THINKING ABOUT THE STORY

1. Write your reaction to this story in a few sentences.

   _____

   _____

   _____

   _____

2. List any words or expressions from the story that are new to you. Find out what they mean and write the meanings in English or in your native language. Also write the part of speech.

   | Word or Expression | Meaning | Part of Speech |
   | --- | --- | --- |
   | _____ | _____ | _____ |
   | _____ | _____ | _____ |
   | _____ | _____ | _____ |
   | _____ | _____ | _____ |
   | _____ | _____ | _____ |

3. What are some serious problems in your neighborhood or city? Have you ever tried to solve any of these problems? If so, what happened?

_____
_____
_____
_____
_____

4. Write a letter to the mayor or city manager of your city. Describe one or two of the problems in your neighborhood or city, and explain what you think should be done about them. Follow the form for writing letters, below.

(your address) _____

_____

(the date) _____

Mayor_____

_____ (your mayor's or city manager's name and address)

_____

Dear Mayor _____ :
    (mayor's name)

_____
_____
_____
_____
_____
_____
_____
_____

Very truly yours,

_____
(your signature)

5. Share your letter with your classmates. As a class, choose two or three of the best letters, correct them with your teacher, and send them to your mayor or city manager. Or, take the best ideas from all the letters and, as a class, write one letter to send to your mayor or city manager.

## FOCUS: GERUND AND INFINITIVE PHRASES

An expression that begins with a gerund is called a *gerund phrase*. An expression that begins with an infinitive is an *infinitive phrase*. Gerund and infinitive phrases function the same way that noun phrases do. Here are examples of two gerund phrases from the stories you have just read.

*Traveling so much* can really be tiring.

The most difficult part of my career is *trying to maintain a private life*.

The gerund phrase in the first sentence above serves as the subject of the sentence. The gerund phrase in the second sentence is the object of the verb.

An infinitive phrase can also act as the subject of the sentence or as the object of the verb. Here are some examples.

*To be a good friend* requires understanding, patience, and compassion. (subject)

*To help clean up a park* is a worthwhile activity. (subject)

The best way to lose weight is *to eat less and exercise more*. (object)

My goal is *to become a doctor*. (object)

**Exercise.** Write answers to the following questions. Use gerund or infinitive phrases as the subjects of the sentences or as the objects of the verbs.

> **Example:** What is the best way to learn a new language?
>
> The best way to learn a new language is *to practice it as much as you can.*
>
> or
>
> *Practicing a new language as much as you can* is the best way to learn *it*.

1. What is the best way to relax on the weekend?

_____

_____

2. What is the most important thing you have done this year?
   _____
   _____

3. After finishing your education, what are your plans?
   _____
   _____

4. What is the most important thing you can do for your child/children?
   _____
   _____

5. What is the best way to find a good apartment?
   _____
   _____

6. What are your favorite hobbies?
   _____
   _____

7. What is your least favorite cleaning chore around the house?
   _____
   _____

8. What is the last thing you do before going to bed at night?
   _____
   _____

9. What is one dangerous thing a person can do in your city or town?
   _____
   _____

10. What is one interesting thing a person can do in your city or town?
    _____
    _____

## PULLING IT TOGETHER

1. Do the following exercises in a group of three or four students.

   a. Read "Rock Star" and "Mayor" in your group. One student will read the first story aloud and another student will read the second story. As you listen to your classmates read, write down any words that you think are mispronounced. Discuss these words after each classmate has finished reading.

   b. Have you ever imagined being someone famous, or having a life totally different from the one you have now? Who do you imagine being, and what is it about this person's life that attracts you? Discuss this with your group, and then write your answer.

   _____
   _____
   _____
   _____
   _____
   _____
   _____
   _____

   c. Imagine that you are that person. Try to imagine all the details of his or her life. Think about the guideline questions below and answer them by writing notes on the lines provided. Then share what you have written with your group.

   1) What were the steps, or the process, you went through to reach the position you have now — education, training, previous jobs?

   _____
   _____
   _____
   _____
   _____
   _____
   _____
   _____

2) What is a typical day like in your life? If your work varies from day to day, describe a typical month or year.

3) What are the advantages of your kind of life?

4) What are the disadvantages of your kind of life?

5) What are your hopes for the future?

_____
_____
_____
_____
_____
_____
_____

2. Now write your story, pretending that you are someone different from yourself and that you are leading a very different kind of life. Use the notes that you made above to help you with details. Write as many drafts as necessary. With your teacher, decide which areas in Appendix 1, *Revising Guidelines,* you should concentrate on at each step in writing your story. You may revise your paper alone or with the help of one or two classmates, according to your teacher's instructions.

3. When you have written your final draft, get together with your group and read your story aloud. Listen to questions or suggestions from your classmates. Make any final changes you think are necessary.

# CHAPTER SIX

# Last Words

In the first lesson in this textbook, you wrote about your feelings as you began a new ESL course. Then, around the middle of the semester, you wrote about how you thought you were progressing. Now, at the end of the semester, it's time to evaluate your entire experience learning English this term. Using all of the information that you have learned about writing — choosing a title, maintaining thematic consistency, paragraphing, punctuation, and so forth — write your final composition, describing this experience. Here are a few guideline questions to help you.

1. Do you feel different about this course now than you did at the beginning or middle of the semester? In what ways?

2. What aspects of this course do you think helped you the most — the teacher, the textbooks, any particular exercises in class, other students?

3. What aspect of the course do you think was the least helpful?

4. Did you have any experiences using English outside of class that helped you improve your English or that changed your attitude about using English?

5. What advice would you give to someone who was beginning his or her first ESL class?

6. As you continue to learn English now, are you going to do anything differently, in your ESL class or outside of it? What will you do differently, and why?

After writing and editing this composition, share it with your classmates. Your thoughts may be valuable to students who will take this course in the future. So think about putting your compositions into a notebook or folder that instructors of this course can pass on to the students who come after you.

# APPENDIX ONE

# Revising Guidelines

## 1. SELECTING A TITLE

The title of a composition can be one word or a whole expression. It is important to realize the difference between the title and the opening sentence of a composition. Both the title and the opening sentence express the general theme of the composition. However, the title is usually one word or an expression rather than a whole sentence.

There are several ways to choose a title for your composition. An easy way is to select the title from the instructions your teacher gives you. For example, if your teacher tells you to write a composition about an important experience in your life, you might choose the title, "An Important Experience in My Life." However, you might want to make the title more specific and choose something like, "My Graduation from High School" or "My First Day in the United States."

It's not necessary to choose a title before you start to write. In fact, it's probably better to select your title after you finish your story and are satisfied with it. After all, you may decide to make changes in the theme or focus of the story while you're writing it. One way of choosing an interesting title is to read over your finished story and find an expression you have used that reflects the spirit of the story. For example, the titles "A Wonderful Boy" and "My Best Friend," found in Chapter 1, come from expressions that the writers use in their stories.

**Exercise.** Read the story titled "My Brother," on pages 102-103. Remember that there is no one perfect title for a story. Think of other appropriate titles for "My Brother," and write them here.

1. _____
2. _____
3. _____
4. _____
5. _____

## 2. THEMATIC CONSISTENCY

When you choose a topic for a composition, you choose a *theme*. It is important to stay with this theme after choosing it. You don't want to write extensively about something related to the theme but different from it. To check for thematic consistency, you can do two things:

1. Read the title carefully. Does the composition as a whole reflect the theme in the title?

2. As you read the composition, stop from time to time to see if you are still writing about the theme described in the title. Have you started to write extensively about something else?

If you find that some part of your composition doesn't reflect the theme in your title, you must either change the title or change that part of the composition.

**Exercise.** Here are two versions of a composition with the same theme. Apply the above guidelines and decide which one has more thematic consistency. Write your opinion on the lines provided on page 100.

## Version 1

### Learning to Ride a Bicycle

When I was seven years old, I wanted very much to learn how to ride a bicycle. I saw other children riding bicycles in my neighborhood, and they looked as if they were having a good time.

Then, one day during the summer vacation I asked my cousin Joe to teach me to ride. He was fifteen, and he could ride very well. Joe said that he would teach me, but that first we had to find a bicycle my size. I didn't have the money to buy a bicycle, but I was able to borrow one from a boy in my class at school.

I remember that my first lesson was on a Sunday afternoon. We went to a park and found a spot where there weren't many people. Joe told me to get on the bike while he held it steady. I started to pedal slowly and he moved the bike. I was a little scared because I thought he was going to let go, but he didn't let go. We practiced like that for about an hour. Then Joe said that we should stop. I was disappointed because I wanted to continue.

Our next lesson was two days later. We did the same thing, but only for fifteen minutes. Then Joe said that he was going to let go of the bicycle. He did, and I was surprised because I continued to pedal and I didn't fall off. Then, I got to the end of the street and I didn't know what to do. I stopped pedaling and I fell off the bicycle. I wasn't hurt, but I was scared. Joe showed me how to move the handles so that I could turn the bicycle. I tried to do this a few times, and I was successful. Then I started to ride by myself. I was so happy that I could ride a bicycle.

I saved money that my father gave me, and in a few months I bought my own bicycle. I was finally able to join my friends in the neighborhood. We rode our bicycles to many different places. We went to the movies and to each other's houses. Sometimes we rode our bicycles to the next town to buy an ice cream. We liked to go to the baseball field about two miles away. That was our favorite place, because baseball was very popular. I liked to play all the positions, but my favorite position was pitcher. I was a good pitcher.

When I was ten years old, I joined a baseball team. We were so good that we won all the games in our division. One time, the local newspaper wrote an article about our team and printed a picture of us, too. My parents were very proud, and they bought many copies of the article and sent them to all our relatives.

## Version 2
### Learning to Ride a Bicycle

When I was seven years old, I wanted very much to learn how to ride a bicycle. I saw other children riding bicycles in my neighborhood, and they looked as if they were having a good time.

Then, one day during the summer vacation I asked my cousin Joe to teach me to ride. He was fifteen, and he could ride very well. Joe said that he would teach me, but that first we had to find a bicycle my size. I didn't have the money to buy a bicycle, but I was able to borrow one from a boy in my class at school.

I remember that my first lesson was on a Sunday afternoon. We went to a park and found a spot where there weren't many people. Joe told me to get on the bike while he held it steady. I started to pedal slowly and he moved the bike. I was a little scared because I thought he was going to let go, but he didn't let go. We practiced like that for about an hour. Then Joe said that we should stop. I was disappointed because I wanted to continue.

Our next lesson was two days later. We did the same thing, but only for fifteen minutes. Then Joe said that he was going to let go of the bicycle. He did, and I was surprised because I continued to pedal and I didn't fall off. Then, I got to the end of the street and I didn't know what to do. I stopped pedaling and I fell off the bicycle. I wasn't hurt, but I was scared. Joe showed me how to move the handles so that I could turn the bicycle. I tried to do this a few times, and I was successful. Then I started to ride by myself. I was so happy that I could ride a bicycle.

I saved money that my father gave me and in a few months I bought my own bicycle. I was finally able to join my friends in the neighborhood. We rode our bicycles to many different places. We went to the movies and to each other's houses. Sometimes we rode our bicycles to the next town to buy an ice cream. We liked to go to the baseball field about two miles away since baseball was our favorite game. Learning to ride a bicycle made it possible for me to do many things that I couldn't do before.

I am very happy now that I learned to ride a bicycle. I still enjoy riding a bicycle.

I think that version number_____ has more thematic consistency than version number_____ because _____

_____

_____ .

## 3. PARAGRAPHING

As you read the stories in this book, you will notice that each is made up of several paragraphs. Paragraphing is the way that writers help their readers understand their ideas.

A composition is made up of three basic parts. The *introduction* lets the reader know what the theme is and why it is important. The *body* of the composition develops the theme and adds detail to it. The *conclusion* gives an ending to the piece of writing; it sometimes restates the theme.

Those three parts should guide you in deciding where to make paragraphs. The introduction and the conclusion are short — usually one to three sentences — and each should be a separate paragraph. The body is divided into several paragraphs, at least four or five sentences long; each paragraph deals with one aspect or subtopic of the theme introduced in the first paragraph. Let's look at several stories to see how they are organized.

"My Best Friend" on page 15 is a description of a person. The outline below shows how the composition is organized and summarizes the main idea of each paragraph. Notice how the writer divides the theme — the importance of her mother — into different subtopics, different aspects of her mother. Each subtopic is described in separate paragraphs in the body.

### Introduction

Paragraph 1: My mother's importance in my life

### Body

Paragraph 2: My mother's physical appearance and personality

Paragraph 3: The special relationship I have with my mother

### Conclusion

Paragraph 4: Restatement of the theme

Some of the compositions in this book are organized chronologically — reporting events in the order in which they happened. In deciding how to divide the body of a chronological composition, think of the length of time that the story covers. Then divide that length of time into units. For example, if the story covers one day, you might divide the body into morning, afternoon, and evening. If the story covers two days, you may decide to write about each day in separate paragraphs. Look at the story "When My Grandmother Died" on page 24. The outline below shows how the writer divided the theme — the day the writer's grandmother died — into different parts of the day, each described in a separate paragraph in the body of the story.

### Introduction

Paragraph 1:   The worst day of my life, the day my grandmother died

### Body

Paragraph 2:   Early in the day: how I found out at work that my grandmother was ill

Paragraph 3:   Later that day: what happened at the hospital when she died

### Conclusion

Paragraph 4:   My feelings about my grandmother's death

"Losing a Friend to Drugs" (pages 59-60) covers a longer period of time.

### Introduction

Paragraph 1:   What happened to my friend Kenny has influenced me ever since

### Body

Paragraph 2:   Kenny's personality and how it led him into trouble one day

Paragraph 3:   The changes in Kenny over several weeks

Paragraph 4:   How Kenny died

### Conclusion

Paragraph 5:   What I learned from this experience

**Exercise.** Here are two compositions written without paragraphing. Read the first composition through once. Then, read it again and make a mark like this [ to show where you would begin a new paragraph. Fill in the outline at the end of the composition with a phrase indicating the subtopic of each paragraph. Remember that introductions and conclusions are paragraphs of one to three sentences, but paragraphs in the body of the composition should be at least four or five sentences long. It is up to you to decide how many paragraphs there will be in the body of the composition. Therefore, you should provide the number of each paragraph on the outline. When you have completed the outline for Composition 1, read Composition 2 and complete the outline that follows it.

## Composition 1

### My Brother

One of the most important people in my life is my brother Richard. He is a good person to me and to other people, too. Richard is twenty-five years old. He is tall and dark. He has long arms and legs. His eyes are black and his hair is black, too. He has a handsome face. He looks very much like our father. He is a very outgoing person. He likes to be with people and to make them laugh. Everyone enjoys being with him because he likes to have a good time. He especially likes to go dancing. He is a good dancer, and when he goes to a club, all the women want to dance with him. Richard is a doctor and he works at a large hospital in Chicago. His specialty is treating children with cancer. Sometimes, when one of his patients dies, Richard feels very sad. But he is very proud when he helps a child become healthy. The children love him because he makes them feel happy. Every Christmas, he dresses up as Santa Claus and brings presents to the children. Richard makes a party for them and they enjoy it a lot. I have always had a special relationship with Richard. He is seven years older than I am. When we were living in our country, he always helped me. I often had trouble with my math homework, and Richard could always explain things to me very well. When I did something wrong and my parents got angry, Richard always made things better. Now, when I have a problem in my life, I call Richard on the phone, and he helps me see how to solve the problem. I am very lucky to have a brother like Richard. He is a wonderful person.

**Introduction**
    Paragraph 1: _____

**Body**
    Paragraph 2: _____

    Paragraph __ : _____

    Paragraph __ : _____

    Paragraph __ : _____

**Conclusion**
    Paragraph __ : _____

## Composition 2

### A Weekend on Long Island

The best weekend I had this year was three weeks ago. I went to visit my cousin Martha. She lives in a big house in Oyster Bay, Long Island. I left Manhattan after work on Friday evening. I took the train to Oyster Bay. When I got off the train, I saw my cousin waiting for me. We drove to her house, and when we got there, I was surprised. I didn't know that she lived in such a big, beautiful house. After I unpacked, Martha and I went to a restaurant with some of her friends. We all ordered seafood. The food was delicious because the restaurant buys fish fresh from the ocean. After dinner, we went to a disco. We stayed there until two o'clock in the morning. Then we went home. Saturday morning, we slept late because we were tired from all the dancing that we did. After eating breakfast, we got into our bathing suits and went to the beach, which was only a few blocks from Martha's house. It was a beautiful, sunny day and the beach was full of people. We had a wonderful time talking to people, swimming, and getting a suntan. We had a quick lunch of hot dogs and soda. Around six o'clock, it started to get cool, so we went home. We took a shower and got dressed. Then we went to my aunt's house, which was about a half hour away. We had dinner and talked a lot about our family and friends. Martha and I left my aunt's house at about 11:00 P.M. When we got home, we watched a movie on television and went to sleep. The next morning, I got up at 9:00 A.M. because I had to get back home and study for a math test. Martha drove me to the train station. When the train arrived, I thanked Martha for a wonderful weekend and went back to the city. That weekend was the best weekend of my year. I hope that I will be able to visit Martha again soon.

**Introduction**

    Paragraph 1: _____

**Body**

    Paragraph 2: _____

    Paragraph __ : _____

    Paragraph __ : _____

    Paragraph __ : _____

**Conclusion**

    Paragraph __ : _____

When you begin a piece of writing, think for a short time about how to organize your writing into paragraphs. When you have finished writing your first draft, you may decide to change the paragraphing some way. If you want to check your own or a classmate's composition for appropriate paragraphing, make an outline of the composition, as you have done in the above examples. Then, with your teacher or a classmate, discuss whether there is a better way to divide the paragraphs.

## 4. PUNCTUATION

Knowing how to punctuate your writing — knowing where to begin and end sentences and where to place commas — depends on your knowledge of sentence types in English. Once you know what a simple sentence is, you can learn how to combine simple sentences into more complex ones. You will then know many different sentence types. When you revise your own writing, you can check to see if the sentences you have written fall into the categories for these sentence types.

First, you need to become familiar with a few terms which describe the elements of a sentence. A *trunk* is the simplest sentence possible, containing at least one subject and at least one main verb. A *coordinator* is placed between two trunks to make them into one sentence. An includer also links two trunks into one sentence. An *includer* is different from a coordinator in that it may come either between the two trunks or before the first trunk. A *shifter* is an expression which adds information about the sentence, often giving details of time or place. It can be placed either at the beginning or at the end of a sentence. If a shifter is removed from the sentence, the sentence is still complete. Finally, a *linker* is an expression that is placed before a single trunk.

| Elements | Examples |
|---|---|
| TRUNK: | subject verb  (Mary cried.) |
| | subject verb *and* verb  (Mary cried and hugged me.) |
| | subject *and* subject verb  (Mary and her brother cried.) |
| COORDINATORS: | and |
| | but |
| | so |
| INCLUDERS: | after           once |
| | although     since |
| | because      so |
| | before         until |
| | even though   when |
| | if                while |
| SHIFTERS: | in the morning |
| | at night |
| | next year |
| | tomorrow |
| | in the United States |
| | in the southern part of my country |
| LINKERS: | after that       nevertheless |
| | before that     second |
| | first                 so |
| | however         then |
| | next               therefore |

Here are the basic sentence types and the punctuation that goes with them. The mark . means that a period must be used. The mark (,) means that a comma is possible but not necessary. The mark , means that a comma is necessary.

| **Sentence Types** | **Examples** |
|---|---|
| Trunk. | <u>I walked the dog.</u> |
| | *trunk* |
| Shifter(,) trunk. | <u>Yesterday</u> <u>I walked the dog.</u> |
| | *shifter*   *trunk* |
| Trunk shifter. | <u>I walked the dog</u> <u>yesterday.</u> |
| | *trunk*         *shifter* |
| Trunk(,) coord. trunk. | <u>I walked the dog</u>  <u>and</u>   <u>Jane made dinner.</u> |
| | *trunk*         *coord.*      *trunk* |
| Includer trunk, trunk. | <u>After</u> <u>I walked the dog,</u> <u>Jane made dinner.</u> |
| | *includer*   *trunk*              *trunk* |
| Trunk(,) incl. trunk. | <u>Jane made dinner</u> <u>after</u> <u>I walked the dog.</u> |
| | *trunk*          *includer*   *trunk* |
| Trunk. Linker(,) trunk. | <u>I walked the dog.</u> <u>Then,</u> <u>Jane made dinner.</u> |
| | *trunk*             *linker*      *trunk* |

The basic rule to remember is that when you combine trunks into one sentence, you must add an includer or coordinator to tie each pair of trunks together. Consider the following example.

<u>While</u>  <u>I walked the dog,</u> <u>Jane made dinner</u>   <u>and</u>   <u>George cleaned the garage.</u>
**(includer)**    *(trunk)*               *(trunk)*        **(coordinator)**        *(trunk)*

There are three trunks in this sentence. The includer *while* ties the first and second trunks together. The coordinator *and* ties the second and third trunks together.

If you are mathematically minded, you can think of this rule in terms of a formula:

The number of <u>coordinators</u> + <u>includers</u> = The number of <u>trunks</u> - 1. (Any number of <u>shifters</u> and <u>linkers</u> can be added to a sentence.)

As an example, in the sentence above, The number of coordinators (1) + The number of includers (1) = The number of trunks (3) - 1.

107

**Exercise 1.** In the sentences below, underline the trunks. Circle the includers and coordinators. Put brackets ([ ]) around the shifters and linkers.

> **Example:**
>
> [Yesterday,] (after) John had breakfast, he looked for his keys, (but) he couldn't find them.

1. We always go to church on Sunday mornings.
2. George had never seen tall buildings until he came to the United States.
3. Before he left, he closed the window.
4. We went to the park to play soccer. Then it started to rain, so we went to a movie.
5. At five o'clock, most people stop working and go home.

**Exercise 2.** Read the following story and put in capital letters, commas, and periods. The punctuated version of the story can be found on page 24.

### When My Grandmother Died

the worst day of my life was the day my grandmother died it was a very sad time for me

I remember that I was at work that day I got a phone call from my brother who told me that my grandmother was very ill I finished my work and went to the hospital hoping that she was still alive

when I got to the hospital my whole family was in the room with my grandmother everyone was crying I went to my grandmother's bed and I talked to her I told her that I loved her and that she was a wonderful grandmother I hoped that she could hear me but she didn't say anything to me two hours later she died

my father told us that we shouldn't be too sad because my grandmother lived a long and happy life however I still feel a little guilty because I never told her how much I loved her when she was still alive

When you check your own composition for correct punctuation, read each sentence separately to determine if it falls into an acceptable sentence-type category. If necessary, diagram the sentences, as in Exercise 1.

## 5. SUBJECT-VERB AGREEMENT

When you write a composition, or part of a composition, in the present, it's important to check the agreement between subject and verb. As you learned in the section above, each trunk in each sentence has a subject and a verb. In the present tense, the form of the verb is different for different subjects. When the subject is the third-person singular — one person other than *I*, one object, or one idea — the verb needs an *-s* ending. For negative verbs, third-person singular subjects go with the form *doesn't*, while other subjects go with the form *don't*. Notice the differences in the verb forms in these sentences.

I *wait* for the Number 3 bus every morning. My brother *waits* for the Number 3 bus every morning. My neighbors *wait* for the Number 3 bus every morning.

I *don't like* waiting for the bus. My brother *doesn't like* waiting for the bus. My neighbors *don't like* waiting for the bus.

**Exercise.** Pretend that you have just written the following paragraph and that you are going to check subject-verb agreement. Identify and underline the trunks in each sentence. Circle the subject and main verb of each trunk and connect the circles with a line. Then ask yourself if the subject and verb agree. Make any necessary corrections in the right-hand margin.

HINT: Keep in mind the difference between main verbs and secondary verbs. Secondary verbs are always in the gerund or infinitive form.

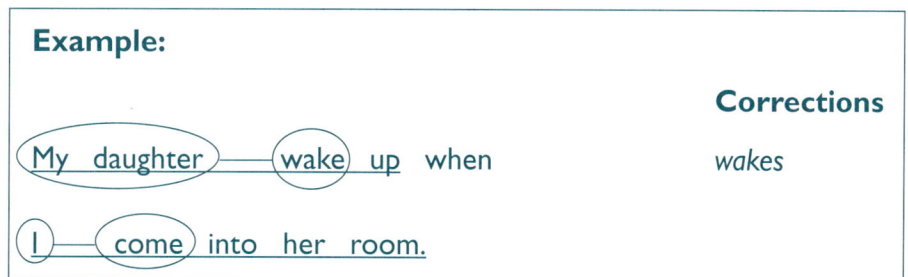

# Corrections

### A Typical Sunday

Every Sunday, my family gets up at eight in the morning. While I make breakfast, my wife help the children while they gets dressed. We eat breakfast together. After we get into the car, I drive to church. My wife don't like the way I drive. She often complain that I drive too fast, but she doesn't drive. The children sit in the back seat of the car. Sometimes they makes a lot of noise. I am happy when we arrive at the church. I enjoy the service. My wife like to see her friends at church. My children enjoys playing with their friends while my wife and I talk to our neighbors.

Use this same method to check subject-verb agreement in your own compositions.

## 6. VERB TENSE CONSISTENCY

After writing your composition, it is important to check the verb tenses you have used. Depending on the theme of your composition, you may use one verb tense only, or you may move from one tense to another. For instance, if you write a composition about a past experience, most of your writing will be in the past tense. However, at the end of the story you might want to describe how you feel about the experience now. In that case, you will have to use the present tense also. Some compositions require you to use more than one tense. For example, you might write a composition in which you compare a school you went to in the past with the school you attend now.

When you use both past and present tenses in one composition, changes from one tense to another will often coincide with a change from one paragraph to another. For a composition comparing high school with college, for example, an obvious way of organizing your ideas would be the following.

### Introduction
    Paragraph 1:  Theme: Comparing my high school to my college [past and present tenses]

### Body
    Paragraph 2:  What my high school was like [past tense]

    Paragraph 3:  What my college is like [present tense]

### Conclusion
    Paragraph 4:  Restatement of theme [past and present tenses]

Paragraph 2, describing your high school experience, would be written mostly in the past tense. Paragraph 3, describing your present school experience, would be written mostly in the present tense. The introduction and conclusion might include both tenses.

**Exercise.** Pretend that you have just written the following composition, which you are going to check for verb tense consistency. Identify each trunk. Circle the subject and main verb of each trunk and connect them with a line. Then check for correct verb tenses, making necessary corrections in the right-hand margin. Finally, complete the outline as you did in the exercise on paragraphing, page 105. Indicate the major verb tense or tenses used in each parargraph.

HINTS: Remember how negatives are formed: *Doesn't* and *don't* are present tense forms, and *didn't* is the past tense form. Also, as in section 5, don't confuse main verbs with secondary verbs, which are always in the gerund or infinitive form.

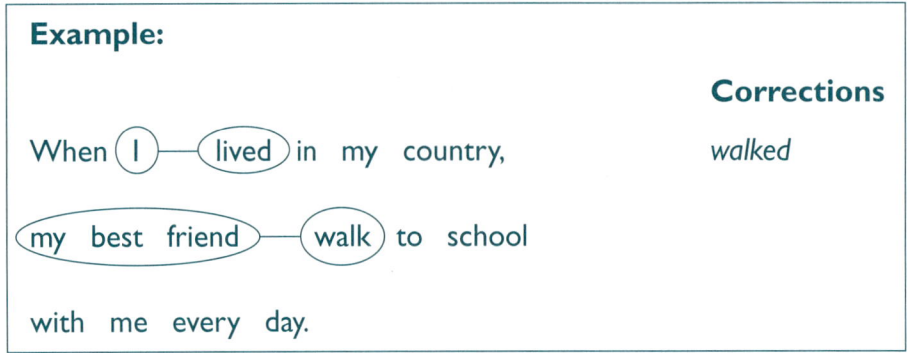

**Corrections**

*walked*

**Corrections**

### Childhood and Adulthood

Now that I am an adult, I see many differences between my life as a child and my life today. When I was a child, I had no responsibilities, but people always tell me what to do. Today, I have many responsibilities, but I can do whatever I want to do.

When I was a child, I have no responsibilities. I didn't have to clean the house or cook. My mother did all the work in the house. While she work, I could play all day. I went to the park or to my friends' houses. We ride our bicycles and went to the candy store for ice cream. We played baseball and basketball. However, there was one thing that I don't like. My mother control many things in my life. She told me when to get up in the morning and when to go to sleep.

# Corrections

I had to come home from school at a certain hour and I have to eat dinner at a certain hour. I didn't like the way that she controlled me, and sometimes I get angry about it.

Now that I am an adult, I had many responsibilities. I have to earn a living so I can buy food and pay the rent. I also pay for my college expenses. When I am not working or studying, I had to clean the house, do the laundry, and cook. However, I have more freedom now than when I was a child. I can get up in the morning and I can go to bed at night whenever I wanted to. I decide what I want to eat. I decide whether to go to a restaurant or to cook at home. If I wanted to go to a movie or to a party, I don't have to ask for permission. I could control my life.

When I was a child, I could do many fun things, but my life was under the control of my parents. Now that I am an adult, I have many difficult responsibilities, but I make all my own decisions about my life. I am happy now that I am an adult.

**Introduction**

Paragraph 1: _____

tense(s): _____

**Body**

Paragraph 2: _____

tense(s): _____

Paragraph 3: _____

tense(s): _____

**Conclusion**

Paragraph 4: _____

tense(s): _____

Use this method to check verb tense consistency in your own compositions.

# APPENDIX TWO

# Supplementary Material

## 1. PARTS OF SPEECH: NOUNS, ADJECTIVES, VERBS, ADVERBS

Throughout this book, there are references to categories of words known as nouns, adjectives, verbs, and adverbs. Here are definitions of these terms.

NOUN: a person, place, object, or idea

ADJECTIVE: a word that describes something or someone

VERB: a mental or physical action

ADVERB: a word describing how an action is done, or a word that modifies an adjective or another adverb

| **Example:** | The | very | beautiful | girl | danced | extremely | gracefully. |
|---|---|---|---|---|---|---|---|
| | | (adverb) | (adjective) | (noun) | (verb) | (adverb) | (adverb) |

**Exercise 1.** It is usually easier to understand grammatical terms in English when you can identify those terms in your own language. Write the words for *noun, verb, adjective,* and *adverb* in your own language. Then list some examples of words in each category in your language. Check your answers in a dictionary, with the teacher, or with someone else who speaks your language.

The word for *noun* in my language is _____.

Some nouns in my language are _____

_____.

115

The word for *adjective* in my language is _____.

Some adjectives in my language are _____
_____
_____.

The word for *verb* in my language is _____.

Some verbs in my language are _____
_____
_____.

The word for *adverb* in my language is _____.

Some adverbs in my language are _____
_____
_____.

**Exercise 2.** Read the words below and divide them into lists according to the appropriate parts of speech.

happy  too  eat  church  slowly  slow
think  marriage  carefully  bored  furniture
computer  fresh  feel  intelligently  big
run  extremely  tall  do  badly  honesty

| **Nouns** | **Adjectives** | **Verbs** | **Adverbs** |
|---|---|---|---|
| | | | |
| | | | |
| | | | |
| | | | |
| | | | |
| | | | |

## 2. NOUN AND ADJECTIVE PHRASES

Sometimes, a group of words acts together as a grammatical unit. For example, the word *boy* is a noun. Look at the following group of words.

the handsome, green-eyed, brown-haired *boy*

These words form a noun phrase whose central part is *boy*; all the other words describe the nature of this *boy*. Descriptive words or expressions may come before or after the noun. For example, look at this phrase.

the handsome *boy* with brown hair

Here, *handsome* and *with brown hair* both describe *boy*.

**Exercise.** Find the noun phrase in each sentence below. Underline the entire phrase and circle the central noun.

> **Example:**
> The big red (house) on the corner belongs to my (aunt.)

1. I have always wanted to buy a big red speedboat.
2. This is my fourth semester of college.
3. New York City has a very special means of transportation.
4. I couldn't come to class because I had a problem at home.
5. The secretary who sits across from me is very nice.

Adjective phrases are often expressions of two words, an adverb and the adjective it modifies.

It is *extremely important* for you to call your wife.

The movie we saw last night was *very interesting*.

**Exercise.** Find the adjective phrase (or phrases) in each sentence. Underline the entire phrase and circle the adjective.

> **Example:** Our teacher is <u>extremely (friendly.)</u>

1. John is perfectly qualified for this job.
2. I am almost finished with my homework.
3. The play Julia acted in was enormously successful.
4. Martin is much taller than his brother.
5. It is never too late to learn something new.

## 3. THE PARTS OF A SENTENCE

There are a number of terms in this book which are used to describe words according to how they function in a sentence. There are two necessary parts of a sentence. The *subject* is a noun, noun phrase, or pronoun. It is the person(s), place(s), object(s) or idea(s) talked about in the sentence. The subject of a sentence needs a *verb*. Here are two examples.

<u>My grandfather</u> <u>died.</u>
   (subject)    (verb)

<u>Jogging and swimming</u> <u>are</u> my favorite sports.
    (subject)     (verb)

There may be more than one kind of verb in a sentence. The *main verb* is the verb that has tense: It tells you whether the action happened already, is happening right now, or will happen in the future. The *secondary verb* does not have tense; it is either in the form of a *gerund* (the *-ing* form) or an *infinitive* (the form of a verb found in the dictionary, with no ending on it). In a sentence, there may be one or more main verbs and one or more secondary verbs. Here are examples.

John <u>likes</u>              <u>to travel</u> to exotic places.
   (main verb)      (secondary verb-infinitive)

I enjoyed         watching that movie and talking about it with you.
(main verb)   (secondary verb-gerund)    (secondary verb-gerund)

We were dancing and talking all night.
   (main verb)        (main verb)

Another important part of a sentence is the *object of the verb*. The object of the verb is a noun or noun phrase which is acted upon by the verb. The object of the verb answers this question: "What or who did (the subject) (verb)?" Here are examples.

The  baby    ate    her cereal  quickly.
   (subject) (verb)   (object)

(What did the baby eat? Her cereal.)

Julie  kissed  Richard.
(subject) (verb)  (object)

(Who did Julie kiss? Richard.)

**NOTE:** A declarative sentence makes a statement. It is neither a question nor a command. The basic word order of the English declarative sentence is SUBJECT - VERB - OBJECT. Compare this with word order in your language. Is there one particular order for sentences in your language, or can the order be changed around without changing the meaning of the sentence?

**Exercise.** Underline and label the parts of each sentence below. Use the abbreviations (s) for subject, (mv) for main verb, (sv) for secondary verb, and (o) for object of the verb.

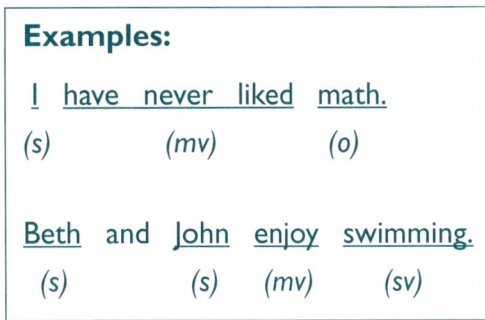

**Examples:**

<u>I</u>  <u>have never liked</u>  <u>math</u>.
(s)         (mv)              (o)

<u>Beth</u> and <u>John</u>  <u>enjoy</u>  <u>swimming</u>.
(s)         (s)      (mv)      (sv)

1. My grandmother and I like to read.
2. George cleaned his apartment and cooked dinner.
3. Tomorrow is the first day of spring.
4. Mary and Julia don't enjoy violent movies.
5. At the beach, we swim, eat, lie in the sun, and have fun.
6. Yesterday, my oldest brother got his driver's license.
7. The big white house on the corner needs a lot of repairs.
8. Many immigrants want to succeed in their adopted country.
9. I will give my children a good education.
10. Janet cleaned the house and fed her baby.

## 4. PRONOUNS

Pronouns are words that can be substituted for nouns. There are four kinds of pronouns.

| Subject | Object | Possessive | Reflexive |
|---|---|---|---|
| I | me | my | myself |
| you | you | your | yourself |
| he | him | his | himself |
| she | her | her | herself |
| we | us | our | ourselves |
| they | them | their | themselves |
| it | it | its | itself |

*Subject pronouns* are used as subjects of sentences.

> **Examples.**
>
> *I* have a new neighbor. *She* is very friendly.
>
> *I* visited my friends in Florida. *They* live in Miami.

*Object pronouns* are used as objects of verbs.

> **Examples.**
>
> My father bought a new car. We like *it* a lot.
>
> I have to pick up my nephew and take *him* to the doctor.

*Possessive pronouns* are adjectives which indicate who owns one or more objects.

> **Examples.**
>
> We're going to take the bus today because *our* car is being repaired.
>
> I live in Chicago, but *my* parents live in California.

*Reflexive pronouns* are used when the subjects act upon themselves; the subjects are also the objects of their verbs.

> **Examples.**
>
> I'm very proud of my daughter. She just learned to dress *herself*.
>
> A cat cleans *itself* often.

**Exercise.** Complete each sentence with the pronoun that refers to the underlined noun.

> **Example:**
>
> <u>My uncle</u> is very important to me. I love _him_ very much.

1. <u>My best friend and I</u> are planning a vacation in Mexico. _____ are very excited about it.

2. <u>Judy's parents</u> want her to get married soon, but Judy told _____ that she wasn't ready to get married yet.

3. <u>John</u> was so nervous about meeting Mary's parents that he cut _____ slightly while shaving.

4. <u>Mr. and Mrs. Gold</u> are going to celebrate _____ fiftieth wedding anniversary next month.

5. <u>I</u> called Mark to ask him if he could drive _____ to my dental appointment on Friday.

6. <u>Martha</u> can't come to class today because _____ children are sick.

7. When <u>we</u> go to the beach, we should always protect _____ from the sun.

8. <u>San Antonio</u> is well known for _____ famous tourist sights, like the Alamo.

9. I would like to call <u>you</u> soon. Can you give me _____ telephone number?

10. <u>Barbara</u> is graduating from high school this spring. _____ hopes to begin college in the fall.

## 5. AUXILIARIES

Auxiliaries are small but important words. Here is a list of auxiliaries.

| | |
|---|---|
| am, is, are, was, were | may |
| will | might |
| would | must |
| should | do, does, did |
| can | |
| could | |
| have, has, had (when in the present and past perfect tenses) | |

You can make a sentence negative by putting a negative ending on the auxiliary in the sentence. The verb that follows the auxiliary is unchanged. Look at these examples.

Sally *is* coming to the party. Henry *isn't* coming to the party.

Mark and Julie *have* visited Florida many times, but they *haven't* visited Texas.

Another important characteristic of an auxiliary is that you move it to the front of the sentence when you form a yes-no question. With other types of questions, the auxiliary follows the question word *(who, what, where, why, when, how)*. Here are some examples.

You *should* see your dentist once a year.

*Should* you see your dentist once a year?

When *should* you see your dentist?

Not all sentences have auxiliaries in them.  When you make a sentence without an auxiliary negative, the auxiliary *doesn't, don't,* or *didn't* is added, and the verb that follows drops its ending, as in these examples.

Margaret *eats* dinner with her parents during the week, but she *doesn't eat* with them on the weekend.

Jerry *wanted* to watch television, but he *didn't want* to watch the news.

When you make a sentence without an auxiliary into a question, you must add the auxiliary *do, does,* or *did* at the beginning.  The main verb of the sentence loses its ending. Look at these examples.

Thomas *goes* to the beach every weekend.

*Does* Thomas *go* to the beach every weekend?

When *does* Thomas *go* to the beach?

**Exercise.**  Circle the auxiliary (or auxiliaries) in each sentence below.  If there is no auxiliary, make a check mark (✓) next to the number of the sentence.

> **Examples:**
> ✓ They tried to get to the theater on time.
> Jane (couldn't) finish her homework last night, but (will) finish it this morning.

1. I like to sit in front of the class because I can't hear the teacher from the back of the room.
2. I have always wanted to learn how to fly an airplane.
3. Could you please pass me the salt?
4. John spent all day yesterday painting the house, and now he feels very tired.
5. There will be a parade tomorrow to celebrate the holiday.
6. If it doesn't rain on Sunday, I might play baseball with my friends.
7. Did you remember to water the plants today?
8. Paul rented an apartment in a very pleasant neighborhood.
9. When she was a baby, Sally liked listening to classical music, but she doesn't like that music anymore.
10. I would like to invite you to dinner next week.

## 6. IRREGULAR VERBS

Here is a list of commonly used verbs which have irregular simple past tense and past participle endings.

| Infinitive | Simple Past Tense | Past Participle |
|---|---|---|
| be | was, were | been |
| become | became | become |
| begin | began | begun |
| bring | brought | brought |
| build | built | built |
| buy | bought | bought |
| catch | caught | caught |
| choose | chose | chosen |
| come | came | come |
| cost | cost | cost |
| do | did | done |
| drink | drank | drunk |
| drive | drove | driven |
| eat | ate | eaten |
| fall | fell | fallen |
| feel | felt | felt |
| fight | fought | fought |
| find | found | found |
| fly | flew | flown |
| forget | forgot | forgotten |
| forgive | forgave | forgiven |
| get | got | got, gotten |
| give | gave | given |
| go | went | gone |
| grow | grew | grown |
| hear | heard | heard |
| hide | hid | hidden |
| hit | hit | hit |
| hold | held | held |
| hurt | hurt | hurt |
| keep | kept | kept |
| know | knew | known |
| lead | led | led |
| let | let | let |
| lose | lost | lost |

| | | |
|---|---|---|
| make | made | made |
| mean | meant | meant |
| pay | paid | paid |
| put | put | put |
| read | read | read |
| ride | rode | ridden |
| ring | rang | rung |
| say | said | said |
| see | saw | seen |
| sell | sold | sold |
| send | sent | sent |
| sing | sang | sung |
| sit | sat | sat |
| sleep | slept | slept |
| speak | spoke | spoken |
| spend | spent | spent |
| stand | stood | stood |
| steal | stole | stolen |
| swim | swam | swum |
| take | took | taken |
| teach | taught | taught |
| tell | told | told |
| think | thought | thought |
| throw | threw | thrown |
| wake | woke | waken |
| wear | wore | worn |
| win | won | won |
| write | wrote | written |

**Exercise.** Divide the list of irregular verbs into groups of ten or twenty words each. Study them, one group at a time. When you think that you know one word group fairly well, try these activities with a partner.

1. On a separate piece of paper, write down five infinitives from the first column. Give the paper to your partner, who will write down the corresponding simple past tense or past participle form without looking at his or her list. Check your partner's answers. Then switch roles. Do this several times. Add up the number of correct answers to see who wins.

2. Make up a sentence about your life in the present tense with one of the verbs on the list. Then your partner will change the sentence to the past tense, without looking at the list. For example, suppose you say, "I sing in the shower every morning." Your partner will then answer, "You sang in the shower yesterday morning." Check to see if your partner is correct. Then change roles. This can be done orally or in writing.

3. Give your partner an infinitive. Without referring to the list, your partner will answer with a sentence about his or her life, using the past participle in one of the following ways: "I have _____ many times." "I have never _____ in my life." "Since I came to the United States, I have often _____ ." Do this five times, checking your partner's answer each time. Then switch roles. Repeat this several times.

## 7. SPELLING RULES FOR ADDING *-S*, *-ED*, AND *-ING*

Here are some important spelling rules to follow when you are adding the common endings *-s*, *-ed*, and *-ing*.

### Adding *-s*

There are two exceptions to adding just the letter *-s*.

1. If the word ends in a consonant and *-y*, drop the *-y* and add *-ies*.

   study      studies

   enemy      enemies

2. If the word ends in *-s, -ss, -ch, -x, or -z*, add *-es*.

   kiss       kisses

   mix        mixes

   church     churches

## Adding -ed

These rules apply only to verbs which are regular in the -ed form.

1. If the word ends in silent -e, just add -d.

    wave      waved
    receive   received

2. If the word ends in a consonant and -y, change the -y to -i before adding -ed.

    marry     married
    study     studied

3. If the word is one syllable long and ends with a single vowel and a single consonant, double the final letter before adding -ed. (Exception: words ending in -x).

    drop      dropped
    fix       fixed

4. If the word is more than one syllable, ends with a single vowel and a single consonant, and is accented on the last syllable, double the final letter before adding -ed.

    prefer    preferred
    admit     admitted

## Adding -ing

1. If a word ends in silent -e, drop the -e before adding -ing.

    change    changing
    write     writing

2. Rules 3 and 4 for adding -ed also apply when adding -ing.

    shop      shopping
    prefer    preferring

**Exercise.** Complete the chart below.

| Infinitive | -s Form | -ed Form | -ing Form |
|---|---|---|---|
| try | | | |
| marry | | | |
| dance | | | |
| kiss | | | |
| match | | | |
| deliver | | | |
| carry | | | |
| mix | | | |
| stay | | | |
| commit | | | |
| order | | | |
| control | | | |
| stop | | | |
| force | | | |
| improve | | | |
| itch | | | |
| select | | | |
| wait | | | |
| answer | | | |
| hope | | | |
| remember | | | |
| travel | | | |

## PHOTO CREDITS

2, Jeff Isaac Greenberg; 5, Michael O. Lajoie; 12, Alex Webb/Magnum Photos, Inc.; 15, Woman's Realm/Globe Photos; 22, Martine Franck/Magnum Photos, Inc.; 24, Michael O. Lajoie; 32, Horst Schafer/Globe Photos; 34, Michael O. Lajoie; 44, Erik Gundersen; 46, Jeff Isaac Greenberg; 50, Michael O. Lajoie; 52, Skjold Photographs; 59, Constantine Manus/Magnum Photos, Inc.; 62, Julie Marcotte/Stock Boston; 72, Eric Liebowitz; 75, Richard Kalvar/Magnum Photos, Inc.; 83, Mark Antman/The Image Works; 86, Reuters/Bettmann; 94, Jeff Isaac Greenberg